A Stone House in Pokhara

AND OTHER TALES

A Stone House in Pokhara

AND OTHER TALES

Mike Frame

Larchill Press
Northfield, Minnesota

Published by Larchill Press
larchillpress.com

Photographers:
Mike Frame, Mary Ellen Frame, Anita Lama, Siddhartha Lama, Claire
Frame, Mickey Veich, Carolyn Young, Surya Kumar Gamal.

ISBN: 978-0-615-51161-0

Book design by Dorie McClelland, springbookdesign.com

This book is dedicated to the people of Nepal,
who welcomed Mike as friend and brother.

Contents

THE LETTERS

ACKNOWLEDGMENTS

Many thanks to Mac Odell and Jim Fisher, both old friends of Mike from Peace Corps days, who did the initial transcription of Mike's handwritten manuscript in the week before he died. Further thanks go to Mac Odell for taking time from his pressing commitments, on three continents, to write his piece about the "honeymoon suite."

I give a huge thank you to Ian Lessing for patiently and cheerfully helping me with technical difficulties whenever I needed help, and for his continued encouragement.

I want to express my great appreciation for the advice, support and encouragement of Glynnis Lessing, William and Sandy Frame, David and Claire Frame, Mary Easter, Sigi Leonhard, Toni Easterson, Beret Griffith, Mary Lewis Grow, Karen Helland, Jan Mitchell and Anne Sovik.

I extend warm thanks to Dorie McClelland for her professionalism in designing a beautiful book, and for her patience with my erratic pace, over a couple of years, in getting the material to her.

Mike laying bricks at Bubbling Springs Farm, ca.1973.
(Photographer unknown)

Introduction

As the title of this book indicates it is, initially at least, about the building of Mike's own house. As Mike's sister, and one who had read and discussed the manuscript while he was working on it, I've undertaken to publish the book. Mike wrote most of the book during the last year of his life; he had hoped to bring it out while he still could. As it was, during the final couple of weeks, fellow Peace Corps Volunteers Mac Odell and Jim Fisher volunteered to type his hand-written manuscript. Jim put it in his hands a few days before he died. None of us was sure, at that point, whether Mike was able to understand that it was done, the beginning of the process of getting it into your hands.

Before Mike joined the Peace Corps, none of our family had ever heard of Nepal; we soon learned it was about as far from home as you could go. Home was a farm near Northfield, Minnesota, where Mike grew up as the youngest of the four children of Bill and Minnie Frame.

On a June day in 1962, Mike got up early to wait on table for breakfast in the college Tea Room, then exchanged his waiter's jacket for a cap and gown for his graduation from Carleton College. In the afternoon of that day, he helped make hay on the farm, and in the evening he boarded a plane for the first time, flying to Washington, D.C. for Peace Corps training.

During his first term as a Peace Corps Volunteer, he taught high school English and Agriculture in Bhaktapur, then Dhankuta. During those two years, he formed an attachment to Nepal and began thinking about ways in which Nepali farming could be improved. After his first term, he signed up for a second, which he spent in the village of Khatare trying out and demonstrating his ideas to local farmers. He then worked in agriculture for two years with U.S.A.I.D. in Janakpur. The chapters in the Letters section contain excerpts from some of the many letters he wrote home during his first four years in Nepal. In those the reader finds expression of his fascination with a country and culture so entirely different from all he'd known before.

In 1969, Mike returned to Minnesota and enrolled in graduate school, studying Agriculture Economics. He was side-tracked from those studies by the opportunity to try out his ideas about farming on a co-operative farm in Wisconsin, that I was also part of. When we moved there, there wasn't adequate housing for the eight adults and seven children who planned to live on the farm. So to get through the first few years, we built an apartment in one corner of the huge barn, then started on a building that would have an apartment for each of the three families and Mike. Building wasn't new to Mike. Growing up on the farm, he'd helped our father in various building and remodeling projects. One summer during his college years, he'd worked as a brick-layer's assistant, so learned a little about masonry. Of mortar he said, "The proportions are the same as piecrust; one part cement, three parts sand, and enough water to hold it together." Mike was the chief architect and brick-layer of the big house. He had very creative ideas

House at Bubbling Springs Farm, west elevation. (Mary Ellen Frame)

House at Bubbling Springs Farm, east elevation. (Mary Ellen Frame)

Dining area at Hotel Fewa. (Mary Ellen Frame)

about designing it, and the practical sense to make those ideas work—most of the time. We re-used a lot of materials that had been part of other buildings that were being torn down. We were dedicated to conserving resources and we hoped to save money as well. But, as Mike said, "Something that's free isn't always a bargain." Nonetheless, the house is unique, beautiful and still lived-in after thirty-five or so years.

In 1980 Mike was offered a five-year term with the Peace Corps as Program Officer in Nepal. He was stationed in Kathmandu, but also traveled around the country, visiting his volunteers and seeing what they were doing. This gave him an opportunity to do a lot of trekking, a chance to see ever changing, ever beautiful countryside and encounter village life directly. During that time he was also thinking about starting a restaurant in Kathmandu. Ever since he had first lived in Nepal, he had enjoyed hosting celebrations, so American holidays became occasions to figure out ways to cook familiar foods without the sort of kitchen he was used to and with the challenge of hard-to-find ingredients. When his tour of duty with Peace Corps ended, he and a Nepali friend began planning to open a restaurant, to be called Mike's Breakfast. It would serve safe, Western-style food in a beautiful setting. Mike planned and supervised the necessary remodeling and the creation of a garden dining area. He trained the cooks and waiters. The restaurant still attracts tourists and resident ex-pats as well as a growing number of Nepalis. Out of this experience grew his first book, *Mike's Breakfast: Cooking in Nepal and Then Some,* part cookbook, part memoir.

He talked about how it would be fun to build a lodge somewhere, where travelers could get a good, safe meal and have fairly clean, basic accommodations. This dream was finally realized when he and partners took over Hotel Fewa by the lake in Pokhara, in 1996. Hotel Fewa gave him an opportunity to do extensive remodeling, even tearing down some decrepit outbuildings and rebuilding them into lovely "cabin" suites. Settling in Pokhara, he decided he could now build his own house—a house that would embody many of his ideas about energy conservation, comfort and use of native materials while incorporating the beauty of traditional Nepali style.

Less than a year after Mike started building, he was diagnosed with Multiple Myeloma. Yet he was able to finish the house and live in it for almost five years. December 21, 2007, was the last day Mike was in Nepal. That morning he and I boarded a Buddha Airlines flight from Pokhara to Kathmandu on our way home to Minnesota. I sat in the seat behind Mike and we both looked out at the Himalayas to the north and the foothills below us. I was very conscious that this might be the last view he had of a country he loved so much and I thought he must be aware of that, too. I imagined him as a young man walking on trails such as we could then see so plainly, visiting the roadless villages, talking with the people he met. On the flight he was silent; whatever he felt I could only imagine.

I hope you will enjoy getting a glimpse of Nepal and of Mike's life there in this book.

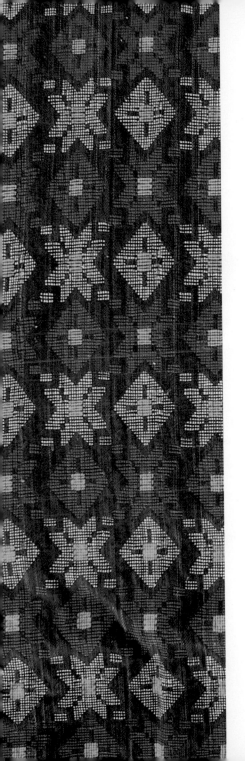

Building

East end of house with pig shed on right. (Mary Ellen Frame)

"Barrows and Gilts—
Nineteen and a Quarter"*

arnie, Profit and Margin have their own room behind the house. Their room is light and airy and is designed to let the winter sun shine in when almost all living souls welcome it. They have a varied diet of local and exotic food catered by Mike's Restaurant at the Fewa Hotel. It tends toward the vegetarian and organic although Profit (we usually call him by his Nepali name, Phaida) shows a strong interest in meat while Earnie goes for the muffins and quiche and Marge, the epicurean, snaps up the quarter pound snails that are tossed his way. It is probably the crunch factor. None of them show much interest in hot or strong flavored foods and have been known to leave an onion or chili pepper on the side of their buffet.

Being barrows, these three pigs show little interest in anything other than eating and sleeping. Sometimes they get a little rowdy, as adolescents will, and do some mock fighting before returning to sleeping mode. Their pen is tidy, with each corner devoted to a necessity of life; eating, sleeping, water, and, of course, the toilet, which for lack of proper facilities, is recognizable for its unusually tidy brown pile and a whiff of the disagreeable.

---

* WCCO Radio "Morning Market Report from St. Paul, c. 1950 quoted in dollars per hundred weight.

I had considered putting in a flush toilet (the squat type, of course) but I couldn't decide whether or not to give the pigs the freedom to flush for themselves or to give their keeper this power and responsibility. It seems a simple problem of political philosophy, but there are real issues here.

First the social issues. Would the pigs decide to each flush for themselves or might this cause a power struggle? Some pig might think he was more equal than the others and want to flush every time. This could lead to flush envy and disgruntlement among the others. Then again, some of the pigs might get lazy about it or not want to flush. There might be a pig that would refuse to use the facility because his "brother" had not flushed before him, leaving an awful mess.

Then there is the problem of information-sharing, such as when there is a water shortage or there is too much or too little water going into the methane generator. It is obvious: we have to keep the power of the flush lever in human hands. Sorry about that, pigs; you shit, we flush.

Putting these flushing issues aside, we were still faced with the a priori problem of knowing where the pigs, given this 10 x 15 ft. space, would decide to shit. There was no way to know this ahead of time although it should have been obvious that the corner furthest from the food trough would be their preference. Now we know, after several generations of Earnie, Shervy, Spiro, W., and Phyda, that each set of siblings picks the same spot even after thorough disinfecting and whitewashing between residents. I also didn't have enough confidence in the pigs' abilities to be precise in their defecations. This is a game of golf, not horseshoes; close doesn't count. Close means the swineherd has to clean up anyway.

As you might suspect, I hadn't yet decided when the masons and their helpers were ready to spread out a huge pile of concrete, with no plumbers in sight and no decision made. The masons put the "moot" stamp on the issue. It was a good job. Now each day the swineherd takes shovel and broom into the pen and moves the valuable resource* from the corner of the pen into the maw of the methane generator to begin another digestion. The pigs are not the only contributors to the methane generator. Sewage from the house (we each do our own flushing) and sometimes dung from an occasional water buffalo calf or steer (which we have been known to raise) are also used to help the pigs provide gas for cooking our food.

The effluent from the methane generator is a valuable fertilizer. The slurry collects in a pair of open concrete tanks and can be used either directly or to make compost when put together with rice hulls and other plant wastes. The vegetables love this fertilizer. The barrows get to go to the restaurant when they are big enough. So do the vegetables.

---

*"A pile of manure is worth money in the bank." W. G. Frame (He usually had more of the former than the latter.)

Houses

had lived in 14 houses in Nepal before I decided to build one for myself. They ran the gamut in style, building materials, and habitability. Of the 14 there were four or five where I lived comfortably, without having a constant desire to radically change or rebuild the house. I always looked for a garden when searching for a house to rent, but affordable houses with gardens were especially hard to find in Kathmandu and Pokhara. When I found one at a reasonable price in the right area, I would decide to rent it almost without looking at the house. I knew I could put up with almost anything if it had a garden to play in. Mistakes were made.

The most comfortable houses were the older ones that were built before the Indian invasion. This change in house design and building methods all began shortly after the highway linking Kathmandu to India was opened in 1959. This invasion was characterized by the sudden availability of steel reinforcement rods ("re-bar") and affordable cement. These materials were accompanied by Indian design and designers and continue to be followed by an army of Indian semi-skilled plumbers, masons, electricians and other of the building trades. The plumber I still call on is from Oriss; the electrician from Bihar.

The last house I lived in was a series of four box-like rooms of

Rebuilt cabin at Hotel Fewa. (Mary Ellen Framc)

brick and plaster with a concrete slab top and bottom. Each room had a window and was quite like an oven in the summer or an ice-box in the winter. Its saving feature was about half an acre of good irrigable farm land that produced great quantities of vegetables for us. I lived in one room with my friend Sukra. The gardener and his wife and two small sons had a room and the other two rooms were used by hotel staff or carpenters. There was also a small shed for use as a kitchen for those who needed it, and a toilet beneath the stairs for those who really needed it.

Now you know what gave me the final impetus to build a house for myself.

For several months I scoured lakeside and adjoining areas; anywhere within walking distance of the hotel. Prices were high for small plots of land. It became clear that for the money I had

Traditional Nepali way of house building. (Mary Ellen Frame)

budgeted there would have to be a choice, either buy the land or build a house. I couldn't do both. Also, for most of the lots even in that price range there would have to be a choice between house and garden. There wouldn't be room for both. I also considered the other side of the lake, but there on the north slope of the ridge, sunshine is very limited in the winter. That would be a problem for both me and my garden.

Then one day I got a message from Munju Gurung, daughter of the owner of the Fewa Hotel. She said she had some land in Male Patan that she didn't want to sell, but maybe I could build a house there. Munju was my savior. We talked and worked out an agreement. I told her the type of house I had in mind , which was radically different from all the other houses being built in Pokhara. Perhaps it wasn't so radical to Munju who had grown up across the lake in a stone house and she had seen the rooms we had built at the hotel. Even so, the fact that she had this much faith and trust in me, before I even had a house plan, continues to amaze and and gratify me.

I quickly got myself some graph paper and started drawing. I'd had a generic house already designed in my mind and all I had to do was flip it over so that the wing was on the left instead of the right. That fit the situation of the land better, although it left the front door not visible from the street. I made a neat copy showing the floor plan of the ground floor and upstairs without mentioning my idea for the subterranean level and had this ready for submission with the application for a building permit.

I really don't think the graph paper was the problem. Munju was helping with this official business and knew enough to hire an overseer in the city government office to draw up a set of plans based on my plans but in proper form. I can only say that the overpaid overseer overlooked my plans except that his plans had some of the same basic dimensions as mine. The building permit came out in due time. The overseer's plan was somehow lost and so we just followed the original plan (almost).

With the building permit in hand, I was ready to start building but there was still some waiting to do. There was a farmer renting the land until the end of the season. Before beginning to build, we had a month to wait until the millet was harvested. So while we wait, I'll digress, and give some background.

Girls bringing fodder from jungle. (Mike Frame)

A House in the Village

In September 1964 I moved into the village of Khatare which was a long day's walk north-west of Dhankuta and a two day walk from the road head in Dharan. I was with the American Peace Corps, assigned to work in agricultural extension with the Department of Agriculture of Nepal. The village leader took me around the village the morning after my arrival and showed me a small, dilapidated, empty house sitting on the north side of about an acre of pretty decent farm land. He said it was mine for two years if I wanted it. I wanted it.

I stayed in the school hostel for a few days with a school master and his wife until I got squared away. The Masterni, as she was called, "impressed" a friend to help her restore the house for me and found a boy to be my live-in, all-around servant. They cleaned, patched gaps in the plaster, washed the 2 little window frames and shutters and door and besmeared the floors with cow dung. The inside and outside walls were of mud and cow dung plaster and covered with a wash of white clay which they repaired. I busied myself with getting a temporary latrine built and got acquainted with the village.

I also built a wood-burning cooking stove from a kerosene tin, with a chimney out of stone and mud. This design I'd

learned about the year before in Dhankuta where Mac Odell
had made one with brick and mud in the house that we shared.
In any village house, I only had stone, no brick to work with,
but I managed to get the chimney through the ceiling and up to
the thatched roof. There I continued, throwing caution to the
wind, with a three-foot cylinder of tin fashioned from a 5-gal-
lon kerosene tin. There was a conflict of interest between the tin
cylinder and a major bamboo rafter, since the chimney was right
in the corner of the house, but with a bit of negotiation and
compromise, there was a breakthrough and the cylinder cleared
the thatch by a good two feet. Somehow the house never burned
down and the stove cooked well. Subsequently I helped some
others in the village to build similar stoves but the idea never
really caught on and people still live without chimneys in their
smoky houses.

The house there had an interior which was 9 by 12 feet. The
downstairs rooms had a height of just over 6 ft, except for the
central beam, which even I had to remember to duck under.
By the entry door, I kept my earthenware water pots. The other
corner on the front had the ladder to the upstairs. The corners in
the back were respectively for cooking and eating. Upstairs the
walls were about three feet high. Above that a well-pitched roof
of bamboo and thatch was the ceiling, which rose to over nine
feet in the center.

At the front of the house (south side) was a low thatched porch
about 6 feet deep with a simple bench against the house wall
where I spent a lot of time, usually with someone to talk to and
otherwise with a book.

The house had no barriers to rats, or insects. For snakes the house had a no-vegetation zone around it and especially in front where the door was, there was an area at least 12 by 12 feet that was packed earth. All houses in the village had that. Rats could be controlled by keeping food and clothing in metal trunks or hanging things from the ceiling. Insects, except for weevils in grain, were no problem since the house, being under the three-thousand foot limit, was sprayed irregularly with DDT inside and out by the malaria eradication project, supposedly done every six months, but they only got my house once during the two years I lived there. They came when I was gone so I couldn't stop them. (It was supposed to be USAID funded.)

This place was comfortable for me. I had a handy latrine. I had a stream to bathe in with a secluded pool just ten minutes walk from my house. I knew everyone in the village—Brahmins, Chhetris, Rais, Limbus, Dhamais, and Kamis (As the Brahmins would list them) and by the end of the two years living among them, I knew how they were all somehow related to each other. The house was perfect for me and I was involved with farming and farmers.

Life was hard for the people of Khatare but no one seemed to notice. Farming, as well as being hard work, was also very complicated, as most outsiders would not expect. A single farm family might own land a thousand feet in altitude above the village, some land around the farmstead, and again some fields a thousand feet lower. This is just part of their insurance policy. Each family would likely have some irrigable land for rice production and other fields with sloping terraces suitable for corn followed

Village house with corn and pumpkins. (Mike Frame)

by millet. When brothers divide up their inheritance, each kind of land is divided and with each generation again divided until subsequent divisions become very small.

Every family with land also kept farm animals. Owning animals was done to produce food, to store and gain wealth, and most importantly, to produce fertilizer for the farmland. The farmers only had ashes, plain manure and manure composted with crop residues and leaves from the forest, as their fertilizers.

Animals need constant attention with food and water and other care every day. They are central to moving soil nutrients from the forests and unfarmed lands through their manure, and recycling farming by-products and household wastes back to the fields to improve rice, corn and other crop production.

Explaining life and farming systems being used in Khatare alone could be a whole other book that I don't want to get into here. Instead, see the flow chart and we'll get on with the story.

Knowing this overwhelming need for fertilizer in the village, and also knowing (rather too well) the health problems associated with the absence of latrines, I decided to introduce a composting latrine. It was a simple affair of two planks laid a foot apart across a hole in the ground 3 feet square and about 4 feet deep. This was surrounded by a vertically placed bamboo mat about 5 feet tall. In the bottom of the hole, I put in some leaves and other plant materials. To one side I hung a branch of my favorite toilet paper plant, which has large, soft, strong leaves and it could easily be replaced because it grew abundantly along nearby trails.

Then it was my daily duty to squat on the planks and cover the evidence with dirt from the excavation pile, where I kept a

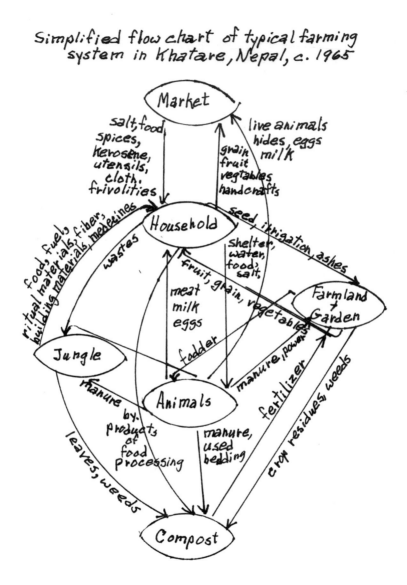

Simplified flow chart of typical farming system in Khatare, Nepal, c. 1965

The farm family also supplied management and labor to all components.

little trowel for that purpose. With a little practice I could hit every spot on the pile of rubble in the bottom. (I was more agile in those days.) When the whole area was covered with dirt it was time to add more litter and continue the process until the hole was full. Then I covered it with more dirt and left it to ripen for a few months.

I had expected that this compost would be wanted by the farmers, since it was a valuable fertilizer. I was wrong. In a society where having a toilet inside the house, as was done in Kathmandu or America, was simply repulsive and disgusting, finding a person to handle this compost was out of the question. Instead, I just planted a small banana plant. This plant grew well for a while and then died. I think it was a case of over-indulgence. Again I went to my neighbor who had a clump of my favorite kind of banana, Jhaji, and got a second sucker. (One can always find a sucker.) This grew quickly into a large healthy plant and within a few months produced the biggest rack of bananas ever known in Khatare. No one objected to eating the bananas.

This home in Khatare exemplifies the traditional houses of Nepal, built with the materials at hand by local people. Certain of these people would gain more proficiency than others at carpentry, stonework, or thatching and be called over by others for house construction or maintenance. They were usually the keepers of tradition, while adding their own innovations to make the buildings more practical, beautiful, and comfortable within the constraints of the situation.

When moving about Nepal, I have become aware of the differences in these traditions. House styles will differ according to the ethnic group, elevation, wealth, social needs, materials at hand, and probably whim. In Eastern Nepal, most of the houses will have a porch on the front. This becomes less common as one goes further west. Also in the east, most of the houses are of stone plastered over with a mixture of clay, cow dung, and rice hulls. Further west, the traditions of stone cutting are stronger and fewer houses hide the stonework with plaster.

I have been referring mostly to the houses of the mid-hills here. The Terai and high mountain areas have their own ranges of style, with wattle and daub used extensively in the Terai, and wood used a great deal more in some high altitude areas.

One house that stands out in my memory was a huge Limbu house just north of the market place in Dhankuta. The story was that Prithivi Narayan Shah, the King responsible for consolidating what is roughly present-day Nepal, made a treaty with the Limbus and Rais of Eastern Nepal (Kirante). In this treaty was a clause that set a tax of one rupee per year on each household. Two hundred years later, this household had not divided. They just kept adding on to the old house and paying the one rupee tax. It was a ridiculous looking house, with rooms added on all around but very few windows. It was said that there were 50 or 60 cooking places for the various nuclear families who were living there and by this time many would be seventh or eighth cousins, hardly related at all but collectively paying one rupee. Most likely they were all still together because they didn't know how to split up anymore.

Waiting for the Millet Harvest

As it turned out, I was nowhere near to starting construction when we got the building permit. I hadn't really decided between stone and brick but I knew that I wanted to use mud as the primary mortar. I still needed to find skilled workers although I had some people who had done construction with me at the hotel. Workers had to be found and agreements made.

My choice of Sukra to act as foreman or supervisor of the project was probably surprising to a few people. About a year before this I had been out trekking with my brother and sister-in-law between Taplejung and Tumlingtar. While waiting for the plane in Tumlingtar to fly back to Kathmandu, I called the hotel in Pokhara. Sukra came on the line and told me, rather matter-of-factly that he had moved out of the room we had shared for two years and moved in with a Swiss woman. This hit me like a bolt of lightning. I could hardly finish the conversation although I did manage to ask him to come to Kathmandu to meet me, which he did. He was easy on me, then, and helped me through my grief. He continued to work as a waiter at the hotel, while building a relationship with Sonya and keeping her pretty much out of my sight. I guess he didn't like that room any more than I did.

Sukra turned out to be a very good choice for foreman. He had helped as a day laborer when we were rebuilding Hotel Fewa so he understood the job to be done, anticipated problems and took action. He was also fair and helpful when dealing with workmen and I knew he would be honest in his bookkeeping. But most of all, he understood me and understood what I wanted.

The carpenter I wanted lived near Hetauda so I called him first thing. His name was Janu Hari so there was plenty of potential for puns. We were waiting for his brother who might be Febru Hari, but no such luck. The brother who came was Nara Hari. No fun there.

Janu Hari had done a lot of work rebuilding the hotel and had made most of the tables and chairs. He came soon after I called, with three helpers, and I installed them at the house I was living in, which was near the building site. I gave him drawings of the windows and doors, specifications for beams, stairway and floor and told him to get plenty of extra one-inch boards. The roof was yet to be decided. He and Sukra spent a few days at sawmills and came home with a huge pile of beautiful wood. Most if it was Sal (Shoria robusta) and pine. Sal is a tropical hardwood rather like our oak in America. It is slow to rot, not favored by insects, very heavy, hard and strong, and finishes beautifully when oiled to a warm, dark reddish brown. Just don't try to put a nail in it.

They immediately set up a work area outside and started planing the wood for the windows and door frames which would be needed first so they could be set in as the walls went up.

With the carpenters working well, I turned my attention to stone and stone cutters. I had decided on stone for the outer walls by this time, since brick would have to be trucked in from Tharpu, a town way down the road towards Kathmandu. I contacted the mason who had done stone work at the hotel and with his help contacted some stone cutters. Then we started our quest for stone and I learned a lot about it.

Most of the stone used in construction in Pokhara is river stone. Only really hard stone survives the ravages of a river and the edges are all rounded off. This stone can sometimes be split into flat slices by experts and then cut with a power saw into various shapes to be used as a veneer on houses with walls made of brick or cement block. This has become the Pokhara style on top of the Indian design.

We would be using river rock for the house foundation and subterranean water tanks, but the stone for the rest of the house would need to be a softer stone quarried from a hillside. We found one site nearby on the ridge just to the west of Pokhara, but the local government wouldn't give the quarry a permit for selling stone, except for local building. We finally found the quarry we wanted on the ridge top beyond Nandara, which is a good ten miles northwest of here. I had previously ruled out brick since it wasn't local and had to be trucked in. Now I was committed to trucking in stone, heavier than brick and with a good portion of it to become useless chips. So much for saving energy.

The stone we would be getting is a light grey sandstone with a slight blue tinge. It would be quarried as needed since the stonecutters find it easier to work when it is still moist from the ground. Actually they like it best during the latter part of the monsoon and just after the monsoon but that was already out of the question.

It would have been good to start bringing in stones and getting the stonecutters started, but there was still millet growing where they would be working.

Munju wanted me to build the house on either the front half or the back half of this long, narrow lot and I decided to build on the front since my neighbor to the north had set his house way back from the road. This meant leaving, on the south of the house, a ten-foot wide space where a lane could someday be built to reach the back half of the lot if a house were ever to be built there. My house would be backed right up to the north wall with only a two-foot gap to service the plumbing and allow space for the eaves to hang out.

Traditional Houses in Pokhara

About six hundred years ago a huge glacial lake high in the Annapurna mountains broke loose. This is not so long ago in geological time nor is it long in historical time since there were probably people living in the valley at that time. There must have been a wall of water hundreds of feet high scouring the upper reaches of the Seti River and bringing millions of tons of rock and debris with it. As I understand it, this immediately created a lake in the Pokhara valley since there was room for the water to spread out and the outlet from the valley was narrow. As the water slowed it dropped its debris with the larger rocks sinking faster than the smaller particles. The Sarangkot ridge, which has a spur running roughly north and south along the west side of the main part of Pokhara town probably protected Fewa Lake and the lakeside area from the brunt of the action and from a great deal of debris that settled, but to the east and south the debris blocked the outflow of Lake Fewa.

As this huge body of water quickly drained it left the sloping plain and started the erosion which made the river and stream gorges that remain such fundamental characteristics of Pokhara. It was also somewhat capricious in the types of debris that remained on or near the surface.

I mention this cataclysm since it is interesting and although I know little about it, it has a great deal of bearing on the construction of houses in Pokhara. Many areas of what is now the city were left with little or no stone nearby for house construction and what stone there was was hard and round. It was to be found mostly in the stream and river gorges, not very handy for building. Other areas had so much stone that the land was no good for agriculture.

It is a bit ironic that in a country so blessed with stone as Nepal has been, many of its urban areas are located where stone has to be transported some distance.

The Newars of the Kathmandu Valley built their cities mainly of brick, since clay for making brick was readily available. When the Newars came to Pokhara they had to look hard to find clay for brick making. It was inferior and not found in great quantities, but they were able to build a bazaar full of beautiful brick houses. Many times brick was used on top of stone when building these houses.

There were also a few brick or stone and brick houses from early times spread around the area south of the bazaar. Before the 1970s, when the road to the outside world came to Pokhara, there were only a few oxcarts for transporting building materials. Otherwise rocks and bricks moved in baskets on people's backs. Therefore most houses built in that period were very small.

If you wander into the area east of Lakeside, away from the lake, you may be able to locate some of the half dozen old houses built in an oval shape that have survived. The oval shape was more efficient than a rectangle in providing more space for the same amount of wall. It was also probably used since most of the stones

Traditional oval house in Pokhara. (Mary Ellen Frame)

Traditional oval house in Pokhara. (Mary Ellen Frame)

in this area were round and hard to cut, making it difficult to make stable right angles for the corners of rectangular houses.

Another peculiarity of this same area in the lower part of Pokhara, which I have not seen anywhere else in Nepal, is the form of wall used between the fields and the trails. Many of these old walls have a facing of stone toward the trail being backed by a ridge of dirt which slopes into the field. Thus the farmers were able to fence out the cattle using a minimum of stone. (In America, farm animals are fenced in; in Nepal they are fenced out.) This type of wall was amenable to growing plants on top that would heighten the wall and hold the soil in place. Often bamboo or poinsettia were planted to good effect.

The trails were made several yards wide, leaving room for the herds of water buffalo and other cattle on their way to and from the lake or the streams. The wide trails also hint that when this area was settled, the land was not highly valued. Would that be because of lack of irrigation, lack of fertility, frequency of hailstorms, Malaria, low population or what? I don't know, but they call the lakeside area *Baidam* which in Nepali could mean "no money" or "lack of value."

Fewa Hotel and some of the other buildings close to the lake that were built before the roads, but after tourists started coming, were built of quarried stone from across the lake. This was a monumental job since at that time they were still using dugout canoes. Those canoes were bigger ones than the few still in use, but still dugouts and made from a single huge tree.

The Planning

Architecture is like cuisine in that very little is ever new. Most of the structures, ideas, recipes have been used for centuries and only tweaked and reshaped with new or different ingredients now and then. I have been an amateur of house design longer than I have of the cooking arts. Being an American living in Nepal, I've had a chance to bring some American cooking ideas together with Nepali ingredients. I've also had a chance to use some Nepali ideas in building a house in America. This house in Pokhara is my first chance to bring together modern and ancient building practices of Nepal with a few ideas from America and other places thrown in.

Building the cottage rooms at Hotel Fewa was my first chance to pair modern and traditional building practices and learn how they can work together or not. These, of course, were hotel rooms and posed some constraints that didn't allow me to use a few ideas that I really wanted to use in a house. I probably could have moved into one of the cottage rooms and been quite comfortable but that would have been too expensive.

Mike and I had talked about the cottage rooms he was planning for a long time. Working an hour or two away on a Kali Gandaki

hyro-power project, and with my wife Marcia living in Kathmandu, I passed often through Pokhara, always staying at Mike's,
of course. Having shared a house in Dhankuta as Peace Corps
volunteers, trekked hundreds of miles together and survived some
wild experiences in Solu Khumbu to be told another day, we rumi-
nated about simple luxuries, fireplaces, verandas, and even double
beds—all things rarely, if ever, found in Nepali hotels, guest houses
or trekking lodges.

True to form, Mike wanted to be different, innovative, and, of
course, welcoming.

Not more than a few months after such a discussion I stopped in
for dinner at Mike's Fewa Hotel. He greeted me with a big grin and
I knew something was up.

"Come see it. My honeymoon suite is ready for you and Marcia!"

And, sure enough, it was just that: A second floor cottage
approached by lovely rough-hewn log steps leading to a charming
little veranda complete with a table and a couple of chairs with a
view to die for out over Lake Fewa, with Machapuchare and the
Annapurnas looming skyward. We then stepped through the door
into a totally charming, warm, cozy room that not only had a
double bed and adjoining bath, but a real live fireplace. Yes, Mike,
you were right: "Mac and Marcia's Honeymoon Suite!" Well, the
honeymoon had been long, long ago, but we certainly felt as though
we were on our honeymoon again every time we stayed there . . .
including our Peace Corps reunion a few years later, when dozens of
our old buddies and their families turned up to celebrate, pay hom-
age to Mike, and remember.

Now, who among us has ever had the honor of having a custom-

*made honeymoon suite to reflect a dream, not just specifications!?
That was Mike, classic Mike.*

    Mac Odell

    January 2011

A few years ago in Kathmandu I lived in an old three-and-a-half-story brick house that was L shaped. This has always been an aesthetically pleasing form for me, but it was the practical feature that won my interest. There were no useless hallways in this large house. The stairwell was in the corner of the L, giving access to most of the rooms on each floor. A couple of rooms were accessible only by going through other rooms or by approaching them from an outside veranda. In many of the houses built in Nepal these days, the house will be split down the center with a hallway running from front to back with rooms on either side that are not interconnected. I see this hallway as a lot of wasted space. That these independent rooms could someday be rented out is probably the original selling point for this design, but I see families occupying the entire house or at least renting a whole floor in such houses with an unnecessary hallway down the center.

    Considering this, I decided on an L-shaped house with the stairway near the corner. The inside width for each wing of the L was to be 12 feet, since that was a limit I set for myself for a concrete slab floor supported only at the edges (walls). I thought that a 15-foot exterior width would look "right," and that would allow the interior spaciousness of a 12-foot room. It was also the limit for length of beams I could easily get for a wooden floor over the living room.

Mac and Marcia's "Honeymoon Suite" at Fewa Hotel.
(Carolyn Young)

On the end of the south wing I decided to have my bedroom upstairs and a living room downstairs. I wanted a large bay window there like the one on the house at Mike's Breakfast in Naxal, Kathmandu. (This is shown quite clearly in the bottom picture on page xvi of my first book *Mike's Breakfast*.) In Naxal, the bay window I speak of seems to have been added on to the original house, because it is set in from the corners of that wing by a couple of feet, and though the bay window is two stories high, the main roof of the Rana-era house is even higher, a high pitched roof over a third (attic) floor. This is where I ran into my first problem with stone vs. brick. The roof on my house would be much lower than this but that would fit nicely with the top of a slightly different bay. Bringing in end walls and then doing a five-sided bay would

Front of Mike's house. (Siddartha Lama)

be easy in brick, but entail a great deal more work in stone. I decided to simplify and bring a three-sided bay directly out from the house walls. This made a more modern look. In the end, the interior worked much better than the exterior, especially with the bedroom upstairs. In the downstairs of the south bay window, I wanted to let a lot of light into the living room, so I put tall plate glass windows in each facet of the bay. These wouldn't be openable since, it being the ground floor, there needed to be some protection from thieves. I don't like metal grills on the outside of windows, so I designed it with closeable doors on the inside, like traditional shop doors that can be closed for shade or security. Each of the three windows are three feet wide, but it would have

Digging the basement. (Siddartha Lama)

been better to have them four feet wide to let in more of the winter sun, and heat. I was designing with the stability of the walls in mind, but as I see it now, I think it would not have mattered structurally and that wider windows would have looked better and worked better.

Building in stone and mud in a land prone to earthquakes puts some constraints into planning a house. The minimum I figure for a piece of wall between windows or between a window and a door is about two feet. Less than that would be unstable without cement. Having less space between floors is also a stabilizing factor. I designed my house with the downstairs ceiling at just over seven and a half feet. Upstairs the walls are about 6 feet with exposed rafters rising to over nine feet at the centers of the rooms.

Another feature of the old L shaped house in Kathmandu that

I wanted was a front porch in the angle of the L protecting the front entrance. This would be a sitting place to watch over the garden and talk to friends. In the village it was the place for the grind stone and for strangers to sleep.

My interest in building a storage tank for rainwater goes back to my childhood where our 1873 farmhouse had a cistern, no longer in use when our family bought the farm in 1943. This was later destroyed, but my interest was revived while living in Kathmandu those many years with water shortages becoming more and more of a problem. It was apparent that every house in Kathmandu should be storing rainwater. In Pokhara, the lakeside area is especially deficient in receiving water from the city system. Many of the restaurants and hotels are dependent on water piped in from springs located on the other side of the lake. Others pump water directly from the lake. There are also some wells.

For the house in Male Patan, I decided to use the foundation walls of the east wing of the house to form a tank for rainwater. That meant running the foundation deeper and making the walls stronger, both thicker and laid with cement mortar. This made a tank of roughly 11 x 20 x 7 ft. Next to this I designed a small basement room for the pump and wine cellar, and a second small tank for storing city water. As it turns out, we have had ample water from the city for all our household needs. We have used the rainwater mainly for irrigating the garden in the dry months. As the city grows, Male Patan may also become a water-deficit area.

Having a peaked roof was a design feature adopted more from my aesthetic taste than for economic reasons, although my economic reasons are not always the bottom line. My economic

Building water tanks in the basement. (Mary Ellen Frame)

reasons also include a desire to keep the money in the local economy by using more craftsmen and local materials than having the money flow out for transportation, cement, rebar and other non-local materials. In any case, a peaked roof fit with my desire to keep the walls low, and fit the rainwater-saving scheme. As it turned out it was both economical and beautiful inside and out. It also saved me from any desire to add on another story, an option that many homebuilders in Pokhara seem to want to leave open.

Another prominent feature you will notice right away when seeing the house is the little dining nook off the west side of the kitchen toward the road. This is an attempted replica of the nook (table number 9) in the old Rana cottage at Seto Durbar (White Palace) where we had the first Mike's Breakfast. It is a favorite spot in the house.

The nook is also a compromise of sorts between the modern western way of a kitchen opening onto a dining area and flowing into a living room versus the old style western way and new style Nepali way of having them all separate. I wanted to have a separate living room, but I liked the idea of being able to sit out of the way in the kitchen and have a conversation with the person cooking. This is also more like village Nepal where the kitchen is the only room for all that happens and a comfortable place to share.

Above and behind the dining nook, set into the north-west corner of the house I put a small upstairs porch under the main roof of the house. I got this idea from a village house (probably Newar) when I was walking the old trail from Pokhara to Kathmandu. I think of it as a gallery for watching the people on the road or watching the Annapurnas at sunset. The porch swing

Dining nook off kitchen. (Mary Ellen Frame)

design comes directly from my great uncle Murray and Aunt Bessie's porch (but made of sal rather than pine).

The rest of the house planning was like filling in the blanks. I knew I wanted some fireplaces. I wanted closets. I knew to put a toilet above a toilet, to put the water heater close to the shower, and in general to have all the intake and outgo of water, including the kitchen sink, in one small area. The upper water tanks that you'll see on top of most city houses, which is needed for storage and to give full-time water pressure posed a problem since I had a peaked roof and didn't really want a water tank spoiling the roof line. I finally decided to put the tank above the lower flight of stairs beneath the roof. That meant not having enough pressure for an upstairs shower. I could live with that; I grew up without an indoor bathroom. Having a big plastic water tank in the

Village of white houses. (Mike Frame)

middle of the upstairs is an indoor aesthetic problem that I have yet to cover beautifully.

Several times I've mentioned the advantages and delights I've experienced with the traditional houses I've lived in. You may wonder why rational Nepali people will, when given the chance, scramble to build the modern Indian style box houses that are going up wherever there are roads. It isn't just the rats. Traditional houses are high maintenance. Floors have to be re-smeared with cow dung frequently and roofs need to be re-thatched every few years. It is also difficult to modernize one's life style in a traditional house. Chairs and tables don't work well on cow dung floors; they gouge and tear up a floor as fast as high heels would. If one wants to change the stove or cooking fuel so that the house doesn't fill with smoke when cooking, there might be insect damage to the rafters and beams without the preservative quality of smoke.

Modernizing an old house with electrical wiring and plumbing can also be a problem. Both wire and pipe are hard to hide in stone walls once the walls are built. Wiring is not a big problem; many older houses have been wired by leaving the conduits and wiring exposed. This is an ongoing and acceptable practice for many. The problem is that it's ugly. Plumbing means a major overhaul, with problems ranging from one end to the other: a tank on a pitched roof, structural damage by leaking water, the need for a septic system. An old house which has been modernized is still a place vulnerable to rats.

So the rush to Indian style boxes continues. Maintenance problems of traditional houses are known. The maintenance problems of the modern style houses may yet be unknown: leaking plumbing, faucets that quit working after one month, paint that falls off damp walls, electrical connections that don't connect, etc.

I could continue on for the rest of the book on the pros and cons of traditional versus modern, but I must say that the main factor in this rush to the modern style is rats. Houses in Nepal are not built just for people to live in; they are also granaries. Especially in the villages and even in towns, to some extent, people store their rice, corn, wheat, millet and other food crops from one season to the next in their houses. There is a constant fight against rats, weevils and other insects in traditional houses. The householders have invented some ingenious ways to carry on the fight. Some people store their corn on poles or racks outside, with barriers to rats under the corn. Some people use hanging baskets.

Ashes can be mixed with a grain to slow down the weevils. Tough wooden boxes have been tried; plastered baskets of all sizes are common. Still, the rats persist. Cement and steel do work. Sheet metal containers are now popular, but for many villagers the containers are expensive and would have to be carried long distances. It is also difficult to provide for the great volume needed to store a whole year's grain supply for even a small family. Sheet metal containers are popular for storing grain in modern houses also because, I'm sorry to say, the rats still get in. They are easier to control, but they do get in.

In the fall of 2001, I brought fiberglass screening from India, since I had noticed that the screen available in Nepal tended to rust out within a few years. I was thinking only about mosquitos and didn't anticipate the fact that rats can gnaw holes and go through fiberglass screening quite easily. Now, after several years of duct-taping these holes to keep out the mosquitos, I find that non-ferrous metal screening is available in Pokhara. Re-screening the whole house should keep out the little critters.

What puzzles me is why this style of building from India has been adopted whole hog. It is re-bar and concrete combined with post-and-beam construction which is filled in with poorly laid brick that needs to be plastered with concrete inside and out. The builders in Pokhara have modified this with a veneer of flat stones cut and fitted in some design, on the front side of the house. This seems almost required now, with a never-ending variety of designs and color motifs. This house dressing is the only apparent modification in this building style I've seen, other than an occasional rearrangement of rooms, or additional balconies and the

Corn attached to a post to keep it from rats. (Mary Ellen Frame)

dangerous practice of having the second story hanging out further than the first.

My question became a desire—a desire to create a house that combines traditional and modern materials, methods and features. It seemed to me that some of the advantages of a traditional house could be incorporated into a design using methods and materials such as cement and rebar where they're appropriate. Cement is especially appropriate in bathrooms; concrete slab floors reinforced with steel, can take the place of wood which has become scarce and expensive. Such a house should be beautiful, economical and keep out the rats.

Building Green

Almost forty years ago I studied economics in graduate school. I find it rather disgusting that economic pundits, and commentators continue to hold economic growth, that is growth in the gross national product (GNP) as the goal of economic activity in a country. It is assumed that higher growth rates indicate that there are lower rates of unemployment and that the standard of living goes up, and all sorts of nice things are happening. But the correlation is minimal at best and rather meaningless. There is also little consideration for the costs, especially the external costs of this growth in GNP.

In China where the growth rate may be 8 or 9 percent, over half the population is unaffected by this in their pocketbooks. They are however affected in the air they breathe and the water they drink. India, also touted for its high economic growth rate and really, the USA also have half their populations unaffected by the growth rate. The rich are the willing beneficiaries of any economic growth.

Lately, a slowdown in the US economy has caused a stir among the economic pundits and politicians. One solution to this problem, the problem that Wall Street has jitters and there are repercussions in the stock markets across the world, is to drop the interest rates. Higher interest rates encourage savings. I don't think Ben Franklin would approve. Tom Lehr put it very well, "Angels we have heard on high, tell us to go out and buy." The second great idea is to send out checks to the taxpayers. The desired effect is that the people getting the money will go out and spend it rather than save it.

It seems the government could have come up with some schemes to spend the money itself, if its concern is employment. They could build high speed railroads, improve other infra-structure, fund research and give incentives for development of alternative energy, build schools, hospitals and houses in New Orleans, etc. but no. This is an election year and the politicians want something quick to please the people and Wall Street.

We must have a new world economic order that discourages long distance shipment of goods, encourages saving, education and health care for all, an appreciation of the environment, and a realistic pricing of natural resources. Such an economics would consider all the externalities in pricing economic activities.

Almost two hundred years ago there was a man called Thomas Malthus. Unfortunately his theories of population growth and the earth's ability to provide properly for these ever increasing numbers of people was discredited and even worse, ignored. Also unfortu-nately the gist of his theories is showing signs of being true. There has been a pandemic of pregnancy around the world. Only the Chi-nese have had any success at a cure. Otherwise churches, mosques and governments are either encouraging the spread of this scourge or withholding information or materials to curb it.

Uncle Warren says: "Global warming will happen just by the

body heat of so many people on earth. If you've ever walked into an old style dairy barn on a cold winter morning, you'd see what body heat can do. The temperature would be thirty or forty degrees warmer inside than outside the barn. Now just think. Each year if we add another few hundred millions of people to the billions already on earth, it is like squeezing a couple more heifers into that barn."

There is a great deal to consider when building a house. The first thing is the quality of the land which may be taken out of production. I hoped the land around my house might become more productive by planting fruit trees and vegetables instead of the corn and millet that the house displaced. Having a source of fertilizer and ample irrigation water would also make the remaining land more productive.

After the land question comes building materials. I wanted materials that were as local as possible, had a minimal effect on the environment in their production and of course were renewable and reusable where possible.

My choice of cut stone for the walls was made for many reasons. Not least of these reasons was the fact that it was traditional but could still be done although other builders in Pokhara were using other methods. I liked the insulating qualities of these walls. I appreciated the beauty. Economically, I was unsure of the costs. As it turned out, with an average of eight men cutting stone for four months and stone needing to be handled in the truckload after truckload from about ten miles away, these costs were less than the alternative. The conventional walls of the Indian style box house have concrete and rebar parts at the corners and at

Mortar in baskets, passed hand to hand. (Siddhartha Lama)

intervals along the walls. The empty sections are filled in with brick laid with cement mortar just one brick thick, then plastered with cement plaster, inside and out, and finally painted again on both sides. Our walls, once the stone was set, were plastered only on the inside with a mixture of clay, rice husks, and cow dung and smeared with a red clay wash for color. This was really cheap since the materials cost little or nothing.

Even had this method turned out to be more expensive, I would have been satisfied because I had used local materials and given employment to a few skilled workers.

Much of the lumber we used was not very local but came from the Terai, which is rapidly being denuded of jungle. It is, however, renewable and there are projects across Nepal which have significantly restored and improved much of the degraded forest.

Village houses. (Mary Ellen Frame)

For the roof of the house I also chose stone slate for its dura-
bility, aesthetic properties, and the fact that it was quarried and
shaped by skilled workers not far from being local. The alternative
would probably have been corrugated metal of some sort. That
would have taken less lumber for support, but one would want a
ceiling under it and perhaps insulation between the ceiling and
roof. So it wouldn't be cheaper than slate supported by wooden
boards, which makes a beautiful ceiling.

For the floors, except my bedroom floor, I stuck to the conventional concrete and rebar being used in other homes being built
today. This has many advantages over the traditional floor, including
a better ability to hold the house together when the earth shakes.

My bedroom floor of wood cost only slightly more than concrete slab. Its main advantage was beauty. It was less sound-proof and the wooden boards keep shrinking as the Sal wood is very slow to dry, leaving wide gaps between the boards. This would also not be a good alternative in general since wood is becoming ever more scarce.

The choice of green materials is, of course, only part of building green. One has to consider the systems that allow the house to help us live lives less dependent on outside energy and resources. I wished I could have put a large solar collector on the roof, but at the time I expected the technology would be changing at a fast pace, making things simpler and cheaper in future. I also didn't have the funds and my expectation of how much electricity we would need was not great.

I did however make my yet unpatented cheap solar water heater. It consists of a coil of black plastic PVC pipe lying in the sunshine, and tied to the bathroom plumbing. One can have a nice hot shower on a sunny afternoon. Who would want to shower any other time? My only place to put this was on the roof of the south porch and surprisingly it didn't work very well. The problem was that the roof wasn't level. Air bubbles would find their way into the coil and stop the water (which wasn't under pressure) from flowing through evenly. A level platform on the porch roof has yet to be built and in the meantime, I installed the smallest electric water heater I could find so when there is electricity available, I can take a shower. It heats in about 15 minutes. The problem is that sunshine is more dependable than 15 minutes of electricity when you want it.

City water in the area where the house stands is quite dependable, so the rain water system with storage tank has not been needed except for irrigating the garden occasionally. I still heartily recommend it for any house being built. One never knows what the water situation will be in the future.

I am especially happy that we built a methane generator rather than a conventional septic system. It has meant that without any problems, we have been able to cook food twice a day for 3 or 4 people for the last five years on the net income. It requires us to keep some farm animals to help us feed the generator. We usually have just the pigs, but if we had more fodder, we could keep a water buffalo and presumably have fuel enough for heating water and even some lighting. We built a simple gray-water system with a small tank to hold some of the soapy water from clothes washing and bathing. We use this water for irrigating the garden sometimes. The effluent from the generator, which comes out as a slurry into two tanks, makes excellent fertilizer for the garden. Sometimes we use this with rice husks for making compost.

As they say these days, it was a no-brainer to put as many windows on the south side of the house as would fit. This has been particularly effective for my bedroom where windows wrap around the bay and heat the room very nicely in the winter time. One flaw here is that the roof is too close above the windows, which shades the top foot of glass even with a low winter sun. That set of windows should have been put in the wall lower down, but my concern at the time of building was the question of supporting a stone wall above there. With hindsight I have realized that a wooden wall could have been fashioned above the windows, which might have looked alright.

Downstairs, in the bay of the living room, each of the three facets has a large window of just one pane which cannot be opened. This has worked well, but once again, if I were doing it over, I would make these windows four feet wide instead of three. That would bring in a bit more heat in the winter time. In the summer, there are shutters to close and other windows to open so the room stays cool.

On the rest of the south side of the house (the east wing) I did what so many non-thinking builders do; I put on a porch. That very effectively shaded one window, reducing the gain of solar heat, although the window still lets a lot of light into the house where it is needed.

Building the House

Early one morning on a clear day in early December 2000, with the Annapurnas getting the first rays of sun on their summits, Munju, with a Brahmin in tow, had us all assembled around a hole in the ground where the cornerstone would be laid at the south-west corner of the house-to-be. Munju, of course, had all the fixings for a proper *puja*, with fruit, sweets, and raksi to finish it off. The Brahmin did his job; the work went well and the house we built is standing nicely.

The next day the trucks starting rolling in. First came a load of bricks and corrugated steel roofing. We needed to put up a temporary shelter for tools and cement and for some of the workers to sleep in. The bricks would eventually be used for interior walls and the roofing would first be used in supporting the slab floors, as they were poured, and finally to roof the pig shed. Then there were truckloads of river rock for the foundation, sand, cement, and quarried stone for cutting.

We also had to find space for all these piles of materials. It was about this time that my knee was giving me a lot of pain and I thought I had arthritis. I thought that maybe I wouldn't want to be going up and down stairs and would want the downstairs bathroom for myself. I decided to make it two feet longer to give me

Brahmin blessing the laying of the cornerstone.
(Siddhartha Lama)

more space and thus the whole house got two feet longer – basement, cistern, and all.

As soon as Dil Bahadur, our head mason, got the area staked out, we hired a couple dozen people to dig the foundation and excavate the area for the water tank. We ended with a mountain of earth on the east side of the work site. Some of the workers claimed to be masons (and had hammers and trowels to prove it) so we put four or five of them to work on the foundation and walls of the water tanks, which were laid up with cement mortar. We soon found out who were actually experienced masons and used them for the most demanding work. There was plenty of work with several truckloads of river stone, which had to be broken up before being used for building the water tanks.

As planned, there were two water tanks. The large one, to be used for rain water, would be 24 feet long, 11 feet wide at the bottom, and 7 feet deep. A smaller tank, only 7 x 7 x 7, would be used to store the city water, which we expected to use and receive on a daily basis, pumping it as needed to an upper tank. There was also to be a small basement room of 7 x 7 which would contain the water pump and the wine cellar. In all the confusion of building, we managed to remember to put pipes through the walls of the tanks about eight inches from the bottom into the pump room. At the center of each pipe, we had an eight inch piece of iron bar welded on perpendicularly so that the pipe could not turn once put in place, making sure that good seals could be had.

Building the tanks took a great deal more time than the rest of the foundation. A floor had to be poured, then the floor and walls plastered with a kind of cement that's impermeable to water.

We also put a layer of this impermeable cement as a cap on all the foundation and tank walls. Another feature of the large tank was to have two brick pillars near the center to help support the floor above where walls were to be built.

From the beginning we also brought in truckloads of quarried limestone and had the stone cutters working. We put them in a large area to the east of the dirt pile. At first there were only about 6 men cutting, but that number increased and varied, sometimes 8, sometimes 10. A few of the stone cutters were blacksmiths so they asked me to buy them a hand-cranked blower and a bag of charcoal. They set up a forge right away and in the evening sharpened their chisels. Two of the men who came to cut stone were young and inexperienced but they wanted to learn so we kept them on and used some of their stones that weren't quite right on the back of the house.

The stones were cut to get the largest face possible out of the quarried stone. Besides the face, the top, the bottom and two sides would need to be squared off while the back would be left rough and as long as possible. The cut stones varied in thickness from 2 to 5 inches and in length up to two feet. An interesting feature is that the stone is cut so that the top and bottom (which are parallel) are not quite at right angles to the face. There is a slightly acute angle at the bottom (only one or two degrees) so that when the stones are laid up in the wall with all the faces plumb, any rain water getting into the cracks between the stones will flow out.

Extra care had to be taken with the stones at the corners. Even next to doors and windows, one side of the stone would need to be cut square three or four inches deep to fit the frames. Our

Stonecutters at work. (Siddhartha Lama)

Siddhartha Lama with the stone cutters forge. (Anita Lama)

Door and window framing set in the walls. (Siddhartha Lama)

Stone masons at work. (Siddhartha Lama)

Living room fireplace. (Siddhartha Lama)

best stonecutter spent most of his time doing the stones for the corners. The obtuse angles on the bay window and around the breakfast nook were especially difficult and, even with our precise geometrical laying out, each of the angles turned out to be unique. I don't understand how that could have happened.

By the time we had the basement work done and the main floor poured and it was cured, we had enough stone cut for the first three or four courses. The first course was laid in water-impermeable cement on the floor slab. Above that we used mud mortar. Dirt that had been dug from the foundation was sieved and then mixed with water using a person's feet to get the right consistency.

One mason laid all of the stones in the outside wall. A second mason worked on the inside wall which would eventually be

Mike with lumber and carpenter. (Siddartha Lama)

plastered over, but even so, required a sound wall. The inside mason used the stone that was not right for cutting, but with great skill, he fit these stones together to produce a wall that would stand on its own merits and be relatively smooth and plumb. The inside and outside walls were raised together and the space between them was filled in with broken stone so that the whole thing was fairly solid.

Door and window frames would need to be set and propped in place as the walls progressed. These were fitted with iron brackets on the sides, which, as the wall came up, would be set into the wall with cement. Above the door and window frames we placed four-inch thick planks extending a foot into the wall on each side, to hold up the stone above. The height of these lintels was a bit tricky to figure. We knew that a wall made with mud mortar

Bay window in Mike's room. (Mary Ellen Frame)

would settle, but we didn't know how much our wall would settle. We didn't want the wall settling so much that the lintel would be resting on the frame so the stone above and to the sides would crack apart. In the end we overcompensated. Our wall didn't settle as much as anticipated so a crack of about half an inch was left between the frame and the lintel. That was easily remedied with a thin strip of wood.

Our wall didn't settle much because the outside mason was using very little mud between the stones, usually not more than one quarter inch. The settling of the inner wall didn't matter so much because the frames were set in the outer wall. Where possible, we built low brick arches over the openings of the inner wall to save wood.

A traditional way of setting doors and windows is to make the

Dining nook on west end of house. (Mary Ellen Frame)

frames with the top and bottom timbers extending a foot or so into the masonry wall to hold the frame in place and to support the wall above. There would, of course, be planks set in behind the top frame timber to hold the rest of the wall. I didn't use this kind of frame because I didn't want thresholds to step over and it would take more wood and the frame might not be so firmly attached to the walls. Actually, I don't remember considering this. I think the carpenter made the decision.

A stone wall like this needs to have the inner and outer walls tied firmly together. This was traditionally done with 18-inch-long stones that were cut on the outside and inside and used every few feet. In our case, with windows taking up a lot of the wall space and the window sills of cement forming strong ties between inner and outer walls, we thought that was adequate for most areas. The brackets holding windows and doors in place, were also cemented in so that inner and outer walls were held together. In other places that we thought might be weak or have a problem, we poured cement in the wall cavity to strengthen those places.

In the middle of the east wall downstairs, I built a fireplace of brick in the inner wall so that the chimney could go directly up in the wall to the peak of the house. We continued upwards using brick for the chimney on the inside while the outside was the cut stone of course. We plastered the inside with mud to make it as smooth as possible and it all worked well.

For electrical conduits we ran black plastic PVC pipes in the floor slabs and up inside the walls to the outlets and switches. This took a little more planning than we were used to and the electrician was a bit perplexed about the whole project, too. The pipe was also used horizontally in the stone walls in places where there weren't impediments like doors and windows. In one case a downstairs light switch was forgotten and we had to run the conduit up and across the ceiling slab when nothing was there to hold it, while the walls slowly rose. That wasn't nearly as easy as running it through the floor. Of course, conduits from switches to light fixtures in the ceilings had to be done that way.

Water, sewage, and grey water pipes also had to be put in the stone walls as we progressed. Having one toilet directly above the other, and the kitchen and water supply being nearby was helpful.

PLUMBERS

As far as I know, there is no simple word for "plumber" in Nepali. A direct translation wouldn't be very realistic anymore either since the plumbers I know don't deal with plumb bobs or with lead (Pb) fittings or work in a plumbery, but it is a plum of a job. Maybe there is more of a relationship to Dick Nixon's friends.

When a plumber is called in, he expects that the masonry work will already be finished. It is preferable to the plumber if the tiling or plastering is all done, but a brick wall with cement mortar will do. The plumber will listen to the householder's requirements, then figure out the longest way to run water from point A to point B. He will then make a list of fittings that will be needed, adding in twenty percent extra of each, because some of them will be sub-standard (but don't worry; he can get rid of the junk later). Then he'll go to whichever store gives him the best commission (but we're not supposed to know about that).

Now it's time for the plumber to draw the lines on the wall where the pipes will be buried. His assistant will gouge out the route with cold chisel and hammer. Then the plumber has time for tea, except if the householder is around, in which case he'll try to look busy, possibly by helping his assistant cut the pipes. The new type of construction, with soft brick and inferior mortar allows the preparation to proceed quickly and neatly. A wall of stone with clay mortar is an entirely different matter. Stones will loosen rather than be cut and the result of this sort of assault will be a mess of rock and dirt on the floor and great gaps in the wall. This too is no great problem for the plumber who, upon fastening the pipes into the gaps, will leave the patching up to his friend the mason. It is a nice life and the future is secure for the plumber, due to the short life expectancy of the Indian-made faucets and fittings.

I hired a plumber named Gagan, whose Shangri-la was

Door in Mike's bedroom. (Mary Ellen Frame)

Upstairs hallway. (Mary Ellen Frame)

Downstairs hallway. (Mary Ellen Frame)

shattered when I suggested to him that I wanted the basic plumbing done before the floors were poured and the walls were built. This was revolutionary. It was a whole new concept in conceptualization. No walls to measure and mark. No wall to hang the pipes in, but only a confusing diagram on a piece of graph paper, drawn by a foreigner.

Putting pipes in the cement slab floors was not so novel or difficult for the electrician who had been running PVC piping for conduits in slabs for a long time. For the plumber it was a little more difficult since it was necessary to estimate the thickness of the cement yet to be laid (plus possible tile) in order to get a proper level for drainage. There was also difficulty in providing for connections to piping that would be put in later in brick walls joined by cement, as described above.

The gray water and sewage systems created more of a challenge. These were to be put into the outer stone walls that would go up slowly and take a couple of months to cover the pipes. At the same time there would have to be intakes that needed to be precise at the first and second floor levels. This is where the mason's plumb bob came in handy. Also, props and guy wires for the plumbing had to be placed out of the way of the stonemasons. It all worked out all right. The masons, with a little effort, were able to encase the pipes in the eighteen-inch wall. They reverted to using cement here and there on the inside to keep it strong. The upstairs toilet seat ended up and inch or two higher than normal, but that's all right for an old man.

Excuse me, I have to pause here; the plumber has come to fix the faucet.

Before we could lay the upstairs slab we stopped the stone work to lay the interior walls of brick. The stone cutters were able to get ahead some as we did this. These inside walls would be laid only one brick thick and when doing this it is only possible to have one side presentable. The back side, considering the quality of the bricks, will be rough and better off plastered. So, before we laid these walls it was necessary to decide which side would show its brickwork and which would be plastered.

Between the living room and kitchen was to be a three-part chimney. There was to be a fireplace in the living room, flue for possible future use in the kitchen and the support for a flue for a fire place to be built in the bedroom upstairs. This also had to be laid up to ceiling level before the upstairs slab could be poured.

When it was time to lay the upstairs floor slab, we laid the inner wall to the level of the bottom of the slab and the outer to the level of the top of the slab. When the slab was poured it rested firmly on the inner part of the wall, was attached to the outside stones, and didn't show.

In the south wing, where there would be a wooden floor above the living room, we had four beams to set in the wall and wondered about leaving the ends open to the outside like you see in some of the old houses. I guess it is to keep the ends of the beams from rotting, as they might if they were covered up by masonry and not given fresh air. The beams we got were not long enough to go all the way through the wall so we scrapped the idea of leaving holes to the outside. The carpenter, Janu Hare, treated the ends of the beams with some concoction of his. Thus, the beams don't show on the outside. On the inside, we supported the beams

Bedroom ceiling. (Mary Ellen Frame)

on a collar of concrete that we poured on the inner wall. This collar went all the way around the horseshoe-shaped room and was reinforced with rods to give extra stability.

Where the bay met the other walls we used a beam heavier than the other three, since in addition to holding up the floor, it would hold up a post in the center, which would in turn hold up that end of the roof. This could all have been engineered differently if the upstairs walls had been a foot higher, six feet instead of five. That of course was out of the question, so we took the simpler solution.

The stonecutters got ahead again while all the work was being done on the floors. That was a good thing since when the stone laying began again that would be several courses uninterrupted by windows that would lay up fast and take a lot of stone. The only interruption was the porch on the North West corner where two

Kitchen. (Mary Ellen Frame)

walls, which would be well under the roof, could be built with brick and plastered over.

The upper story went up without a hitch since everyone knew his job by then. I was the one with the problem, which started out with a sore knee, but turned out to be Multiple Myeloma, a form of bone marrow cancer. On my last day in Pokhara, in mid-April I went over the plans for the inside walls with the mason and told the carpenter to put on a temporary roof of corrugated metal. There was, in all, quite a bit of work they could do without me. The carpenter could finish putting doors and windows in the frames. The masons had walls to build along the road and property line. Sukra went with me to Bangkok so Bishnu, my partner and manager of the hotel, agreed to manage the rest of the project.

When I returned in the fall (November, 2001) there was still

Living room. (Mary Ellen Frame)

Upstairs porch with swing. (Mary Ellen Frame)

View from upstairs porch. (Mary Ellen Frame)

Downstairs porch. (Mary Ellen Frame)

enough work left to do to keep me busy all winter. Floors and some ceilings had to be plastered. The bath and a half had to be fitted. Walls had to be plastered and colored. The temporary roof had to be replaced. One upstairs wall was wrong and had to be rebuilt. A hog house had to be built and tons of stone chips and dirt had to be moved to make a proper landscape.

The stairway had proved a challenge for the carpenter. Most stairways in modern houses now are made of cement. Mine would be made of wood, and we had left space in our building for a squared, U-shaped stairway to be fitted. I finally got the lumber I needed for the side supports and marked them myself. Then there needed to be a couple cut on the diagonal (almost triangles) to get around the corner. This had been hard for the carpenter to conceive. But with some wide boards that we had, it turned out beautifully.

When we started cutting stone I had no idea how many chips would be left over. There turned out to be plenty; after sitting in one place for about a month a stone cutter would find himself on a pile of chips three or four feet high. He would then move to another place and create a similar pile of chips. When we were to build the pig shed, we decided to bury some of these chips underneath. We dug out the good dirt about three feet deep, ten feet wide and 25 feet long. We filled that with stone chips and still had plenty left. Next we did the same with the area by the gate that would be the car-park. After that, we hid some under the front porch and under the walkways. What was left, sadly, got mixed into the soil which was to be our garden.

By then I had decided on using slate for the roof but found there was really no local slate supply. We found slate near Dumre on the road to Kathmandu. The carpenters got busy taking off the metal roof and redoing the rafters. Slate is much heavier and the rafters had to be closer together. I had decided to let the rafters show on the inside and not install insulation and a proper ceiling which would have been the choice if we had gone with a corrugated metal roof. The rafters were then covered with one-inch boards and above that I planned to have a layer of tar paper. Well, the tar paper we found was really a tarred fabric, loosely woven jute that was dusted in fine sand after being tarred, to keep it from sticking together. In any case, we used that over the boards, but I wonder at its effectiveness since there were many holes in it.

Slate goes up a lot like our shingles although they are not tapered from the top to bottom. This can be compensated for by nailing a half inch think strap of wood around the perimeter

Koursani Phul in full bloom. (Surya Kumar Gamal)

of the roof which will give the bottom slate the same slope as those above. It is surprising that the slates don't all shatter when nailing through them, but very few do. The slates we used were fifteen inches long. They are overlapped, leaving about five inches exposed, so there is quite a bit of redundancy built in. Just two nails at the top secure each slate. Sometimes the roofer uses an extra heavy nail or punch to put the holes through the slates. The first nails we used were coming through the one-inch board ceiling of the room below so we quickly changed to shorter nails.

Just as with other shingles, we used sheet metal in the valleys, on the ridges and around the chimneys. Our only problem with leakage has been around one chimney and it hasn't been enough to send someone up to fix it.

While the roof was going on, there was plenty of work to be done inside. First the slab floors that were left rough had to be plastered so they could be used as finished floors. There was also plastering to be done on the downstairs ceilings, which had also been left rough. The downstairs bedroom ceiling where the workers had been careful with the corrugated metal support did not need plastering. We just left a corrugated ceiling.

After all the cement plastering was done and dried, we started plastering the walls. This was done with a combination of clay, rice husks, cow dung and water.

I'd hired a couple of women specialists for this and along with a couple of boy helpers they did an excellent job. Two years later it is as good as new. On the surface of this plaster we smeared *rato meto,* light orange clay. The clay was mixed with water and carpenters glue which keeps the clay from brushing off on peoples' clothes.

From then on the finishing up seemed to lag. There was still painting to be done, kitchen cabinets and closets to build, built-in and free standing furniture to be made, bathrooms to finish, curtains to hang, wood work to oil, screens to fit on the windows, eves troughs and downspouts to make, a simple solar water heater to make and a few other things to do that I've forgotten (some still forgotten).

I was able to move in just before I left for America in May.

Earthquakes

The first earthquake tremor that I ever felt caught me with my pants down. I was in Dharan, having just had some fun with a friend when the rumbling and trembling came. At first I thought it was related but then I realized it was an earthquake. We grabbed our clothes and ran out in the street like everyone else. After a while in the street we went back inside figuring that was all there was to it, just like our relationship.

The house we were staying in was probably safer than most in an earthquake. It was a wooden house on poles that went deep into the ground. Such a house can shake a lot without being shaken apart. The main danger is getting hit by a falling tile from the roof. One might be safer by staying inside rather than running out, but in Nepal instinct tells us to get out.

The second time I felt a tremor, I was in Kathmandu, in bed again, but alone. I jumped up and ran to the door and found that it was raining really hard outside. I paused in the doorway, not wanting to get wet. Since the earth didn't shake again, I just stood a while longer in the doorway ready to run and watched the rain. What a dilemma: a slight chance of a house falling on me versus a sure chance of getting wet and cold in the rain. I stood there trying to decide while the slight chance diminished.

Those sorts of tremors, I understand, allow the release of some of the pressure building up in the earth's crust, and may help delay or lessen the major earthquake that is coming. The Himalayas continue inexorably to rise and the land occasionally has to shake. Every hundred years or so a major earthquake has hit the Kathmandu Valley. The last big one was in 1934 so, given the margin of error, the next could hit any time.

A hundred years is time enough to forget some of the lessons that might have been learned in the last earthquake about building houses to hold up when given a good shake. But fifty or sixty or even seventy years is really inexcusable. Most of the builders of today pay little attention to the possibility of an earthquake. There are some things to remember and lessons to be learned from the old homes in Kathmandu that have survived an earthquake or two. In some of these old houses, built of mud and brick, I have noticed features that include thick walls (at least 2 feet at ground level), small rooms, low ceilings, small windows and floor joists that are square in cross section. The last feature I found quite interesting since in America, most of the joists are 2-inch planks, set up on edge. This will provide more load-bearing capacity for the same volume of wood. Tip them on their sides, however, and there won't be much strength at all. A square floor joist can roll with an earthquake without losing any strength. (For you Kathmandu old timers, there was more to learn in the Momo Cave than the qualities of *raksi*. That's where I became fond of boiled tongue, too.)

Low, small, dark rooms are not going to sell well anymore. Engineering and architecture have come a long way since that was necessary, and many "earthquake-proof" buildings are being built now especially in Kathmandu. But not enough! I seriously fear for these people who are living in that house of cards called Kathmandu.

In the house I was to build, I didn't consult an architect either but I was only going to build it two stories high. I started with a heavy foundation. The L shape was also more stable than a simple rectangle, especially with the bay on the south wing. The downstairs floor was a single reinforced slab that went to the outer edge of the foundation. Upstairs the slab (except above the living room) sat on the inner foot or so of the wall and joined the cut stone on the outside, filling in the gaps around the stones. Below the beams of the living room ceiling, I used rebar and concrete on the inside foot of the walls to solidify that horseshoe-shaped feature. Several other places were also reinforced, and of course below all the windows, there are concrete sills joining the inner and outer walls.

The roof is another matter. It is a simple style with beams down the center resting on the end walls and inner walls and in one case, a post. Rafters were then laid between the beam and the outer walls. These were joined above the beam (to the rafter on the other side) and set well into the walls. All this was covered with one-inch boards, and again covered with slate. So the roof is really just one piece, the wood and nails giving it some flexibility. So an earthquake would likely leave it in one piece, although fallen in places. There is also the question of what the slate would do.

In an earthquake of 7 or 8 on the Richter scale, my house would probably fall down like those around it. I do feel that it would be safer because it is low and well built. The advantage is that much of the wood could probably be reused, and the stone is cut and ready to be used again.

Social Change

When I first came to Nepal (in 1962), I noticed that men were holding hands with other men, boys with boys, girls with girls, just all very nonchalantly. I didn't get into this right away, but as I made friends, they were soon taking my hand and it felt very nice. I hadn't done this in Minnesota. When sitting around, in Nepal, boys could be seen caressing and embracing each other, and as long as it was with the same sex, nobody paid any attention. Except for family members, touching someone of the other sex was simply not done.

This all baffled me for a while. Could all these people be gay? In a way they were. They didn't have the homophobic constraints that most of the world has and they were just acting naturally within the constraint of not mixing with the opposite sex.

There is no word for homosexual in Nepali that I can find. Without a word, the concept was practically missing also (except for some of the temple sculptures). They had it right! We try to categorize people, put them in groups, put them in boxes and label them because of a trait that isn't just one trait. Sexuality is an individual thing. There is a continuum of people's sexual preferences from what we can call homosexual at one end, through bisexual to heterosexual at the other end. But this explains little.

Sexual preference can extend to body type, race, age, hair color, skin color, species, or just about anything imaginable. Sometimes gender is not even a factor.

In Nepal, without a category or concept of gay, there was also apparently no homophobia. Imagine a young gay man growing up not having a label for himself, but still finding that he was different in wanting to go further in affectionate behavior than his friends, whom he could sleep with at will. He might or might not find someone compatible. The question of marriage was there, and in most cases a gay man would do as his family expected, get married and father some children. Occasionally, a gay man would have by this time an idea of his sexuality and perhaps a repugnance for marriage. He might extend his studies or just move away, making some excuse like employment.

In the late 1980s gay groups started forming in Kathmandu and other towns. Some of the members were fairly militant and wanted to follow the gay rights agenda of Western countries. The difference in situation between gay Nepalis and their counterparts in the West was seemingly overlooked. The gay movements in Western countries in the early stages were mainly an attempt to overcome homophobia. In Nepal, although an awareness of homosexuality had crept in through TV and cinema, there was still little awareness or homophobia in the general population. Thus, the Nepali gay groups had to first inform the Nepali people that there was such a thing as homosexuality before they could fight homophobia.

It is very rare now to see two young men walking down the street holding hands. The first part has seemingly worked, the second part will probably take a lot longer.

Mani Rimdu

When I was living in Khatare, Mac and Barbara invited
me to be with them for the Mani Rimdu festival that
would take place at Chewang Monastery near where they lived
in Paphlu, Solu-Kumbu. I decided that since I'd been to Solu a
couple of times by the normal route through Bhojpur and Okhaldhunga, I'd try a more northern route that looked a bit more
direct on a map. The only problem was that the maps I had didn't
show many trails in that area.

I packed my *jola* (shoulder bag) with my usual change of clothes,
skimpy towel, toothbrush, soap and razor, *khukuri* knife, sleeping
bag and more food than I'd usually carry. I spent the first night in
Tumlingtar which was luxurious compared to what I had coming.
In the morning I crossed the Arun river in a dugout canoe and
headed west on a trail that followed a tributary of the Arun and,
according to my map, headed in the right direction. At nightfall I
found a farmhouse where the family let me sleep on the porch.

My third day out was not so straightforward. There were many
trails that divided where there was no one to ask the way. When I
did find a person, I would try to get as much information as possible for my next few hours of trail. In the late afternoon the trail
I was following divided several times until there were only traces

Views of a Sherpa house. (Mike Frame)

in any direction. I had been told that I would need to cross a big stream here, so I followed one of the paths down to the stream. This was no small stream that I could skip across. It had plenty of velocity, depth and width with boulders scattered about. I walked up and down the stream for awhile looking for a place to cross, but I could see no possibility. Night was falling and a light rain also began so I found an overhanging bank by the stream with just enough room for me in my sleeping bag.

In the morning I decided to go back up the hill until I could find someone to help me. It didn't take long. I found a man watching over his rice field in the middle of the jungle. He took me back to the river and showed me a way across, hopping from boulder to boulder. This was not far from where I had spent the night. He also told me how to find the trail on the other side and how I had to go for most of the morning.

That night I found a mill by a small stream in the middle of the woods where I curled myself around the silent millstone. There must have been houses in the area, but it had been a day or more since I'd seen a house. The following day brought larger trails and villages and that evening I got to Paphlu and the warm welcome of Mac and Barbara and the family they lived with. The trip had taken five days, the same as if I had taken the usual route.

I was just in time for Mani Rimdu so the day after I arrived we made the climb up to Chewang Monastery which sits above a high cliff just to the north of Paphlu. It seemed the whole village was going up to Chewang with groups of people singing and laughing and having a good time. When we got there, we settled into some nice rooms and looked the place over.

In the evening when I was getting ready for bed I had a message that Ang Gyale wanted to talk to me. Ang Gyale was a young man in his early twenties and a member of the family Mac and Barbara lived with. I had met him on a previous trip and liked him. That evening he had had a drink or two, and knowing that I was a friend of Mac, wanted to tell me his feelings about Mac and Barbara. It was the classic love triangle and I had been caught unawares.

Ang Gyale told me how he really liked Mac and respected him but he didn't like some of Mac's mannerisms and his interactions with Barbara. Ang Gyale was in love with Barbara. He resented the fact that Mac and Barbara were living in one room and obviously were lovers. To Ang Gyale, this sort of thing was bound to spoil Barbara's reputation. This all went on for some time and finally I got away by promising to talk to Mac and Barbara and him in the morning.

It wasn't just the morning. All the next day was spent sitting in the balcony, drinking salt tea, eating Tibetan breads and of course watching the monks dance in their fantastic costumes. Every few minutes though this was interrupted while I went outside with one of the principals: Mac, Barbara or Ang Gyale.

Mac had a plan to leave Barbara and his work in Paphlu and get a transfer to the school in Namche Bazaar. He had met the head master of that school who had invited Mac to come teach there. Mac, of course, would need to be officially transferred by the district education office and the Peace Corps and that would take some time. He also wanted to say his goodbyes to his students and friends in Paphlu.

Barbara was a person who loved the world. She had a love for everything that lived and because of that, people would easily have a fondness for her. It was hard for her though, to sort out her loves for Mac and Ang Gyale. She loved Mac and didn't want to hurt him and didn't really want to be separated from him, but maybe she loved Ang Gyale more and wanted to make a life with him. In the end, she decided that she couldn't have both, and would go with Ang Gyale.

With Ang Gyale, I talked of Mac's plan to leave but told him that it would take some time to make a gracious exit. Ang Gyale wanted him gone right away, but he agreed to give Mac some time if he separated from Barbara.

By the end of that day, I had had numerous cups of tea and pieces of bread and short periods of watching the dancing and had walked and talked in the garden with each of the principals several times. It seemed that all had been decided; Mac would leave for Namche Bazaar as soon as possible and Barbara and Ang Gyale would be free to get married and go on living in Paphlu.

I went to bed that night tired from a day's work and feeling confident that everything would work out. Sometime after midnight, Ang Dunde, Ang Gyale's older brother and I were woken up. Ang Dunde was to go to quiet Ang Gyale who was in a rage and I was to go to Mac who was the object of that rage.

The problem had all developed because Mac had been very interested in seeing the Sherpas do a rare line dance and had asked Barbara to let him know if this happened. Then Mac went to bed and a while later Barbara and Ang Gyale came in, bubbling about the great line dancing they had just taken part in. Mac was quite upset with Barbara for not informing him. I expect that Mac gave her a good dressing down for what he thought was quite important, while she professed that she hadn't thought it was important at all.

Ang Gyale was incensed by this and decided that this was the last time that Mac would chastise Barbara in public—and was also sure this meant that Mac still had not let go and harbored a grudge against Ang Gyale's relationship with Barbara. This was when Ang Dunde and I were called on to keep the peace.

I found Mac, who was really frightened, and decided to go back to Paphlu, get some things and head off to Namche Bazaar, where he'd been offered a job teaching in the Hilary school. I was not to tell anyone where Mac was. We heard Ang Gyale had a *khukuri* knife, then we heard that he had a gun and was vowing to kill Mac.

Meanwhile, Mac had slipped away in the moonlight and he told me later that he had reached the house and was packing his gear when he heard Ang Gyale out in front of the house shouting and shooting off the gun, calling Mac to come out. Mac tied a couple sheets together and slipped out the back window and was on his way to Namche. I expect he was running the first few miles; in fact he must have run most of the way to Namche because he made it in just a couple of days instead of four.

Back at the monastery, I decided that since sleeping was out of the question, I might as well start off for Kathmandu myself to report all this to the Peace Corps office as Mac had asked me to do. There was a full moon (great how these festivals fall on full moon nights) and I knew the trail was good so I set off about two o'clock that morning.

Compared to the trails I had been using getting to Paphlu, this was like a super highway. There was only one patch of snow about thirty yards wide on one pass and my not having shoes was not a problem; I just ran barefoot. I could count on easily finding places to eat and sleep. Usually during the day the food was *dahi-chura,* (yoghurt and beaten rice) and if there was *achar* (chutney) or an egg to fry, I'd be quite happy. In the evening I would find a tea-shop or house I could sleep at and usually a good supper.

Since the moon comes up later each night I would stop at sunset, find a place to eat and sleep, and pay my bill. That left me able to leave when I woke in the middle of the night and be on my way again. I was in a hurry. I reached Dolal Ghat on the Sun Kosi river my third day! That has got to be some sort of record.

The next day I made a mistake. Instead of taking the old walking trail which would have gotten me into Dhulikhel in half a day, I trudged along the Chinese highway then being constructed. I had hoped to get a ride on a truck at least part of the way, but the Chinese didn't like Americans in those days and just passed me by, leaving me in their dust.

At the Peace Corps office the following day I found out that the Director had gone out to visit me in Khatare. This would be a problem. I told the Deputy Director the main features of the happenings in Solu and of Mac's need to transfer to Namche Bazaar where he would soon be already. I then arranged for a morning flight to Biratnagar and went shopping. A big tin of peanut butter would come in handy.

The last leg of my rather circular trip was pretty familiar; a flight to Biratnagar, a rickshaw to the bus station, the bus to

Dharan and then a hike to Dhankuta. There I stayed with a couple of Peace Corps friends that made me comfortable and rested for my final, all-day dash to Khatare.

As I rounded the last turn in front of my house, I saw the Peace Corps Director, George Zeidenstein, sitting on the porch. He had also just arrived so my not being there was no big deal. He was interested in getting more Peace Corps Volunteers working in agriculture and since I was the only agriculture volunteer working in Nepal at that time, he wanted to know what I thought about it. We talked far into the night. I don't recall what we did about supper.

Tale of Calcutta

One morning at the Red Shield Guest House in Calcutta, I was sharing a table with a couple of Peace Corps Volunteers who were working in West Bengal and a young American traveler. The latter was monopolizing the conversation, telling how he was flying here and there to see the latest ruins and recently discovered ancient temples. He seemed pretty disenchanted with India, telling the company at the breakfast table (who seemed quite comfortable living in India) about the horrors of going out into the streets and mingling with those filthy people. He was particularly upset and apprehensive this morning because he couldn't get first class accommodation on the train to a nearby "place of interest" listed in his guidebook. Finished with my breakfast, and tired of listening to this windbag so full of himself, I was about to excuse myself, when he turned to me and asked, "Have you ever traveled second class on one of these Indian trains?" "No," I told him, in all my honesty and innocence, "I've only gone third class."

Another morning at the Red Shield, the conversation turned to what could or could not be found to buy in Calcutta. I said that I wanted to buy a pair of Jockey shorts but I doubted that they could be found. One of the volunteers who worked in a town not far from Calcutta and knew the city well took up the challenge.

He said they could be found somewhere in Calcutta but it would take some digging. The bet was a twelve-rupee steak dinner for two at the Grand Hotel.

I had been eating regularly at a not-so-nice Muslim restaurant, where I could get wonderful beef curry and a pile of *parathas* for one rupee. I was ready to improve my living standard for one evening, at least, and it was beef that I wouldn't be having back in Nepal.

The search was on for Jockey shorts. We went all over the city to the big markets, the small markets, the clothing stores and the stalls on the streets. He took me around by bus and trolley, asking shopkeepers in his limited Bengali for this precious thing called Jockey shorts. They had no idea what "Jockey" meant; why this insistence on "Jockey?" Wouldn't a locally made pair of shorts do? When they said they didn't know, we quickly moved on. There was a lot of territory to cover.

Late in the afternoon, when we were about to give up, we found a pair of rather shop-worn Jockeys, but they were far too small for me. We decided to call it a tie and split the cost of the sirloin. He showed me the way back to the Red Shield, which I would never have found on my own.

We put on our best clothes, such as they were, and presented ourselves at the Grand Hotel. As I remember it, the meal was delicious, the service impeccable, the company congenial, and the dining room elegant. Best of all, for six rupees each, the price was right!

The
Letters

Village houses. (Mike Frame)

INTRODUCTION

The first part of this book was written by Mike in his later years. As the book developed, I decided that a great addition would be to include some of the letters he wrote in his youth, chronicling his introduction to Nepal, his early experiences there. It was a place, life and culture he could not have previously imagined, nor could we, the recipients. The letters create a vivid picture, which could not come from any other source. He wrote to our parents almost every week, usually completely filling the flimsy little blue aerograms. Whenever one of them arrived in the mail, from either him or our brother, David, who was a Peace Corps Volunteer in Sierra Leone, it was welcomed with great excitement.

The early letters tell so much about first impressions. I've tried to select the most interesting letters and portions of letters—those that tell a good story or describe events and practices that are particularly characteristic of Nepal. He tells about his joys and frustrations and the people he got to know. There are also passages that illustrate his developing skills in farming and cooking. I've edited these lightly, letting Mike's personality come through.

Mike engaged his parents and others in his projects, asking our mother for recipes and asking our father to send agricultural advice, information, pamphlets and magazines. He appreciated all letters from home and especially packages with American food and other hard-to-find items. He had already begun to make connections between the place and people who had always been home and the new home he was finding on the other side of the world.

Mary Ellen Frame, editor

Kathmandu and Bhaktapur, 1962-63
LETTERS

September 24, 1962
Delhi, India

Dear Folks, I guess I didn't quite make it to Kathmandu like I said I would. We went out to the airport, went through Customs, had our baggage loaded, waited for an hour, then went through Customs again after our baggage was unloaded, then came back to meet the rest of the people waiting on the hotel steps with their luggage. The visibility in Kathmandu turned out to be zero so we didn't leave. Then we worked on getting transportation for the rest of the weekend. There appeared three alternatives for getting there: 1. Wait for limited space on Indian airlines flights, since they couldn't charter another plane for us, 2. Charter a plane from the Nepali airlines, 3. Go by train, truck and foot (or, it was suggested, on elephants.) We chartered a Nepali airplane to be here Monday, but it never arrived—probably poor weather. We sent ten out this morning on Indian airlines, and some will leave Wednesday and Friday by plane and the rest will leave Wednesday night by train. I happen to be in the latter group. We will have a forty-hour train ride—third class—then switch to a meter-gauge track until we reach the rail head, then load into busses, trucks and jeeps as far as possible, and finally walk for seven hours where the roads are impassable. It should be fun. Anyway I was slightly afraid of the Nepali airlines, which was a possibility, since they have the worst flight record around, after crashing two of their three planes this summer.

In Delhi I'm having a pretty good time just looking around and playing in the traffic. I would say that the traffic here is the wildest in the world. Today we rode across town in a three – wheeled taxi with five narrow escapes from complete crack-ups and almost ran over two bicycle riders. There is every conceivable type of transportation on the street. Everything from the most modern car or truck to two-wheeled carts pulled by a buffalo or cow and carrying a load of Coca-Cola bottles or hay or most any-thing. The girls here are really quite worth looking at also.

I have not taken many pictures here; I hate to take my camera along because it is so conspicuous. . . . I hope to get some shots of traffic and people here before I leave.

The other day we went out to a government experimental farm. They are working primarily with fodder crops, legumes and grasses. They have developed an excellent herd of native cattle, which they milk by hand four times a day. They also have a herd of buffalo. However the buffalos give more and richer milk. They are bigger and seem to have better udders. Dad, would you send me some statistics on your cattle such as herd average, best cows, etc.? These people sometimes ask these sorts of things and it would be nice to give them accurate answers. I am becoming a great tea drinker here—breakfast, lunch, supper, mid-morning and mid-afternoon tea. I had about ten cups today. Otherwise I only drink a coke every couple of days.

I have been reassigned to another town—Dhulikel, not far from Banepa. I have no idea whether this assignment is more authoritative than the other. The setup is about the same.

Love, Mike

September 27, 1962
Kathmandu, Nepal

Wednesday night, when we were all in the lobby of the hotel with all our luggage, they told us we couldn't go by train due to a bridge which is periodically submerged in water. We were then able to charter two more Nepali airlines flights, so that I arrived here yesterday afternoon and the remainder came in today. The flight was just beautiful. The weather has somehow cleared up so we could see the snowy peaks of the Himalayas on our way in. The mountains are fantastic, then the wide green Kathmandu Valley was really beautiful. After all our talk about the Royal Nepal Airlines, this flight turned out to be the smoothest flight so far. I took a few pictures on the way but they may not turn out very well since I couldn't depend on the light. After all my bother, I only got two pictures of Delhi—the fort, which I toured one day, which contained a beautiful palace with ingenious waterways, and a band which was practicing at the fort under a tree for the festival next week. When I was sitting under a tree with the band, I had

View of Nepal from airplane. (Mike Frame)

tea with them. Then I talked with several people. After that I left with a boy I met there and he showed me all over Delhi. First we walked to the river which was flooding, then we got on a bus. There were two men who kind of tagged along. They were going to take me to see some dancing girls. Pretty soon the bus stopped and blew its horn for ten minutes then shut off its motor. Then we got out and walked ahead and found that for half the block all the cars were coming from one direction and the other half the block all the cars were from the other direction. They may still be like that. We walked on into what seemed to be a grain storage area. This time there was a traffic jam of carts piled high with sacks and pulled by bullocks. If there is anything unmanageable it is a pair of bullocks! Think of a street completely full of them!

Then we got into some old narrow streets, perhaps eight feet wide which curved all over between three and four story houses. We then had tea and climbed up two stories to see the dancing girls. As I expected when I saw the stairs, the dancing girls turned out to be one prostitute. Beautiful girl, but she wasn't boiled. She called after me as I hastened away. Anyway this boy got a big laugh out of it and we picked up a two-man taxi and left the others behind. I brought the boy back to the hotel with me for tea in the afternoon.

Delhi was exciting but Kathmandu is really lovely. This morning we got our shots of gamma globulin for hepatitis and then got our bicycles. In the afternoon we rode out to the airport to greet the last Peace Corps Volunteers to arrive—two miles. We are staying at the Royal Hotel (a former Rana palace,) where the food is delicious—much better than Delhi. There is no traffic here like there was in Delhi—only a few cars, trucks and jeeps. There are no carts pulled by animals here. We ride our bikes all over the streets, but we have to go very slowly and watch for people since they walk all over the streets. However they are very friendly and if you hit one of them they just smile and laugh at your inability. I rode down just before supper and bought a *topi* cap to wear.

Saturday morning
It looks like another beautiful day here. My Nepali instructor is taking us out to our village today. I have been reassigned to Bhaktapur, which is six to nine miles away. The schools are about to start a two-week vacation so we will stay here at the hotel for two weeks for our training. I haven't used much Nepali yet except to

the waiters. In Delhi I was beginning to learn a little Hindi. Much is the same in the two languages. . . .

Kathmandu is approximately what I expected, three and four story brick houses divided by narrow, winding streets, with temples and shrines built in every corner. The shops are all open and go in about ten feet in the bottom floor of the houses. The people here are better clothed than they were in Delhi. I don't know why I keep comparing Kathmandu and Delhi; they are completely different. Kathmandu is just a large small town of 100,000 people, not so many vehicles, and the pace is slower. I must now go eat breakfast, then we have a meeting, then out to see my school.

October 5, 1962
Kathmandu

Dear Folks,
Well, today is the time I sit on the stool again; yesterday I avoided it all day, but the day before I averaged ten-minute intervals. I guess the water here has quantities of minerals which they used to use for a laxative back in the States, at least that's what our doctor said. Nothing to worry about yet. I haven't received any letters yet, nor any of my freight. They estimate another two to three weeks for air freight and January or February for surface freight. Did you receive my cards from London, Beirut, letter from Delhi, Kathmandu? . . .

We are still in Kathmandu at the Royal Hotel. We have four hours of language each day and lectures by the A.I.D. people the

rest of the time. I have attended five receptions in the last four
days. Yesterday was the big one on the Ambassador's lawn. All the
cabinet ministers were there. We had already met the Secretaries of
Agriculture and Education, and the Ambassador before. What was
best yesterday was that I got better acquainted with Mr. Cazely who
is the A.I.D. man in charge of developing vocational education in
Nepal. He told me a few things about Bhaktapur, where I will be
going. Bhaktapur is one of the three or four schools in Nepal where
there is already an agriculture teacher. This means I will not have to
start from scratch and write my own syllabus. Also there are only
three classes of Ag. students and only one where I will be doing
even half the teaching. So I expect that I will be able to start slowly
and learn a lot before I start teaching. There will be an eight-week
Ag. training course this winter for preparing Nepali Ag. teachers at
the College of Education here in Khathmandu which I might be
able to attend. So things look quite a bit better than when I first saw
the farms, which are managed entirely differently from what I have
known. All labor is done by hand. Today I saw the first horse-drawn
cart I had seen since I left Delhi. Almost everything is carried on the
back or in baskets hanging from a yoke diagonal to a man's shoulders. When they carry these they are trotting along with short steps
in such a way that the baskets don't swing or go up and down; they
are very graceful with their huge-muscled legs.

Saturday some of us went out to Bhaktapur and saw the town
and our house. It is four and a half stories, brick, brand new with
hand-carved lattice in the windows, etc. The interior is mostly
natural wood. From the penthouse and roof porch you can look
out over all the house tops in the village and see the entire valley.

Street in Bhaktapur. (Mary Ellen Frame)

But—no running water or toilet facilities, but there is a big old brick and moss-lined well about five feet behind the house. Bhaktapur is very old. Some of the buildings were there at the time of Christ, and are lived in, in the same manner. The widest street I saw was about twenty feet wide. (Not counting the squares.) Most will barely let a car pass between the houses on each side. There are temples all over the place. Also chickens and children. The school looked like a pretty tolerable place, a fairly new, large building set apart from things. Since our house was brand new, there were peacock feathers over every door to keep out evil spirits. Some of our furniture was in the living room so we sat down and ordered some tea and boiled eggs. The ground floor was built with doors opening all around and would be used for a shop or stable if we were Nepalis. We may keep a few chickens or just keep the bottom floor as a working place and garage for our bikes. Our bikes were made in India and everything is going wrong with them. Presently mine has two flat tires, which I haven't had time to fix all week. The road to Bhaktapur isn't too bad (paved halfway) so I will be able to make the eight-mile trip often by bike.

Sunday night the Ramsdells [uncle and aunt of Tom Nelson, Mike's college roommate] had a few of us out for dinner. The A.I.D. people live quite well (three servants) with better houses, furniture, and food than most people in America. We had imported "deer meat" which was the closest thing I've had to beef since getting off the airplane. Also real ice cream. Yesterday at the Ambassador's we had orange juice, which really tasted good. You can't imagine how you can miss some of these things.

The farmers are beginning to harvest the rice now from fields

Pottery shop. (Mike Frame)

which are deeply ditched for drainage. Whole fields have been tied in bundles for some time to prevent lodging. One day you see a field of rice standing on this rough, ditched land and the next day you see the land already completely worked level (to prevent loss of moisture) and seeded to a winter crop. Each little field is perfectly level—perhaps half an acre at the largest. Then there are two to three-storied, small, brick houses sticking up right in the middle of the rice fields and a path leading there which separates the precious rice by only a foot. On all the walls and fences are growing squash and pumpkin vines. On Sunday we also went out to Patan where there is a Tibetan refugee center. They were busy making rugs, etc. by hand, starting with uncarded wool. Very beautiful workmanship and very happy, friendly people for being refugees.

We expect not to have any electricity or water in the hotel in a couple of days because the border of India is closed now and there won't be any more fuel shortly. The border disputes with exiled Nepalis living in India have been getting worse, I guess.

Please give my address to the "Voice," Mom, which I would like to get, also anyone else. Dad, if you see anything on poultry or simple tool ideas which I could make, this sort of thing would be handy in my work. There are two welders in the valley, also I might make my own forge for making tools. The weather here has been mostly cloudy so far, so I haven't taken any more pictures. . .

Love, Mike

October 14, 1962
Chandeswori Home
Tibuckchhen Tole
Bhaktapur, Nepal

Today was my first day of school teaching. We moved to Bhaktapur yesterday and boy, what a deal. We have two floors of a brand-new, four-story house. It is not quite finished yet, so the carpenters are still running around and will build a stove yet, put in some ceilings and put in a bathroom. The house is built of brick with hand-carved wood in the windows and doors. The interior is mostly beautiful wood, except some of the walls are plastered and some bedroom floors are dried mud. We are trying out a cook, mainly because it is so hard for us to do the marketing, and he seems to be good although not too cheap by their standards. It

is rather funny; people are always running around and looking at
everything. I guess they are our neighbors. It was especially interesting to them yesterday when we moved in.

Today I went to school and found out the deal. I will be
teaching two periods of sixth grade Agriculture. Until the two-
month winter vacation I will be working together with the present
teacher since the students have only started studying English in
the fifth grade and I will have to teach in Nepali. But [Nepali]
is their second language, since everyone in town speaks Newari.
Bhaktapur has about 37,000 people and over ninety percent
of them farm the land around town. All the people seem very
friendly and happy. I have never seen people smile so easily. My
students seem very young, but they seem ready to learn. Since
Nepal has been open to foreigners and their strange ways for only
about twelve years, they are quite ready for learning new tech-
niques. We can see great changes just beginning in technology.
It is sort of exciting. We see Shop, Home Economics and Agriculture being taught in the schools for the first time, side by side
with Sanskrit, the link with the past. I will be teaching six days a
week, and will have Saturdays off. Also, they have many holidays.
The *puja* holidays [Desain and Tihar] are now just over after two
weeks. They are the biggest. I took a couple pictures out on the
parade grounds where all the goats were being kept. One boy
wanted so badly to have his picture taken with his great big goat
and when I went to take it, other boys came running from all over
to have their pictures taken. The goats were all to be sold, then
they would be slaughtered in or in front of the temples. Almost
every family has a goat to eat except the poor, who find a chicken

Boys with goat. (Mike Frame)

a great treat. I watched a buffalo calf being killed. One blow from the large knife took the head clean off. I got up too late to see the goats killed.

I expect my air freight to arrive any day now. It took sixteen days for a letter from David [in Sierra Leone] to get here. I keep thinking of things I should have sent, such as bouillon cubes, dried milk, etc. Mom, I would just like your special recipes because we have a cook book. Dad, I would appreciate any information you might have on bee-keeping, vegetable growing and poultry. Perhaps, if you know of some good magazines on those subject, you could write them and ask them if they might send me a free subscription. These are the things I will be working with most. . . .

October 30, 1962
Bhaktapur

Dear Mom and Dad,
I've been getting so many letters but I haven't written because I
couldn't get hold of any aerograms and letters otherwise are just
too damn expensive. I received my ballot [for U.S. election] when
I was in Kathmandu Saturday and sent it in yesterday after showing it to some people who were interested. It cost me 3 rupees,
which is more than double this [letter] and when you consider
that we pay our cook about 2 rupees a day, it comes to quite a
bit of money. Some college students were quite interested in the
ballot, wondering what all the offices were for. Just last week
there were elections here for the city *Panchayat*. Since most of the
people here are illiterate, they receive a ballot, go into a tent and
put the ballot in the box which has their candidate's symbol on it.
You can see where it would be almost impossible to elect ten or
twenty officers at a time like we do.

I am sitting out on our roof this morning enjoying another
holiday. I guess this is the holiday time of year. Quite a bit of the
rice is already harvested now and it appears to be a very good
crop. The nights are very cold now so the morning sun really
feels good. We can see some of the Himalayan peaks almost all
the time now. It's very peaceful and quiet here. We can hear the
birds and dogs and quiet sounds of carpenters and children and
chickens, coming out of the windows of houses, but only once
every hour or two the sound of a jeep or truck coming through
town. The poinsettias in the garden across the street are beginning

Mike and boys on roof. (Photographer unknown)

Farm with mustard in bloom. (Mary Ellen Frame)

to bloom; they grow ten or fifteen feet high here. Yesterday I
wrote to William's and Mary Ellen and planted some flowers in
some pots up here. I also went for a walk and took two or three
pictures. One I took hastily on the road was of the backs of a very
colorful group of men carrying home their rice. The man in the
lead had two baskets of rice hung from his pole, all decorated with
flowers and a sugar cane sprout sticking up out of each basket.
The men were very happy, singing and trotting along. It was probably the first or the last or perhaps all of this family's harvest.

The other day at school I learned that since I am here to help—
me being an agriculture expert—the land behind the school, seven
or eight acres, which has in the past been rented by peasants,
will now be managed by the school and worked by laborers. The
school hopes to get more revenue in this way, and to have it be
a model for the community to follow. It looks like quite a bit of
work for me, but a real chance to be doing something. The plan is
to have a poultry house, vegetable plots, fruit trees and also rice,
wheat and corn, for the students to work with. Also we will continue to raise peppers, mustard and sugar cane, for profit. By the
way, here they raise mustard for the oil. It looks the same as our
weed mustard. I would like to get hold of some bees, which won't
be too hard after I get some materials on how to care for them.
They might help to increase the production of mustard, peppers
and flowering vegetables. Also there are so many flowers around
that a sizeable amount of honey could be had for the asking.
There is no winter lay-over here either. I may also try to get some
swine and goats to work with. There are quite a few razor-backed
pigs in town that are the worst looking things I have ever seen. I

doubt if they have ever been fed anything but garbage and what dung and other things they can pick up in the streets. However, they do help to keep the streets clean. Only the lowest class people eat them. The ducks and chickens here look pretty good. After a field of rice has been harvested, the chickens or ducks are turned in, depending on whether there is or isn't water in the field. . . .

Love, Mike

November 17, 1962
Bhaktapur

. . . Tuesday, the night of the full moon, the people had a harvest festival. In front of different temples, they would make pictures on large mats out of grain, popcorn, beans and pastries. I started wandering around, looking at the beautiful things and a shop-keeper from up the street started showing me around and telling me all about everything. We got along quite well, although he didn't speak any English and he showed me places and temples I never dreamed existed, in back alleys and courtyards. There must be about a thousand temples in this town. We walked for two full hours and still heard chanting and saw lights down alleys where we didn't go. The chanting was done from old Sanskrit books, to drums, bells and all sorts of peculiar instruments. Every little group in front of a temple had its own way of worshipping. In front of one, two men sat at attention in chairs with lamps burn-ing on the various horizontal portions of their bodies. . . .

November 20, 1962
Bhaktapur

Dear William and Sandy,
. . .We seem to be having more holidays than we have school
days. Last week my sixth grade Ag. class, which meets the last two
periods in the day, only met twice because we had three half-
holidays and one full one. The holidays are rarely announced and
sometimes they are only found out about when only a few people
show up for school. The system seems to be similar to what David
has described so well [in Sierra Leone.] But the high school is one
of the five multi-purpose high schools in Nepal and has recently
introduced Ag., Home Ec. and Shop and will be getting a good
supply of tools from His Majesty's government. There is also a fair
amount of good science equipment, which has been locked away
in the school library. The library consists of five or six cabinets full
of books, which are permanently locked. Two of my roommates
are going to make a workable library out of it during the winter
vacation. I expect to go to the Ag. workshop at the College of
Education during the two-month "Christmas" vacation. There we
will prepare the seventh-grade textbook and syllabus.

So far I haven't really done very much. I taught the seventh
grade class one day when the other teacher wasn't there. It was
really a chore but it was worthwhile for me at least. I found a
microscope locked in the library, got an onion and showed them
some plant cells. Then I wrote what I remembered of the photo-
synthesis formula (simplified form) on the board and described
it in my best Nepali—stopping to look up words in my little

dictionary. It was kind of fun, although most of them were laughing at me before I was finished. I found that drawing and writing on the board is the best way for me. They can understand quite a bit of written English but hardly any spoken. The boys seem very interested and anxious to learn and the teachers are devoted, but somehow they can't get together. Only forty percent will pass the exams and this is determined quite a bit by luck. . . .

The people of the town seem to be getting used to me or else I am getting used to them. Anyway they don't seem to stare at me as much as they used to. But anything we do is talked about all over town. I went into Kathmandu Friday and came back before school Sunday morning on my bike. I had so much stuff that I bought a basket and tied it on my bike. This is not a common practice, so when I got to school, the other teachers had heard that I had come back from Kathmandu with a basket on my bike. Most of the Newari people carry everything in baskets hung from the ends of a pole across their shoulders. The Tamangs (people from the surrounding hill regions) constantly come through town carrying things in packs slung from their foreheads. Some carry eighty pounds on their backs in this fashion. . . .

December 4, 1962
Kathmandu

Dear William and Sandy,
Some people here are not too happy with the [education] system and are anxious to learn about ours. It is mostly the English system

as imported from India. In the high school the students take notes
on about eight subjects all year long and then memorize the notes
and write them word for word in the three-hour exam at the end
of the year. Otherwise there are no tests and no homework. The
students really don't need to think very much. It is especially bad
in math and science where everything is taught every year. Arith-
metic, Algebra and Geometry are taught on alternate days. A
typical exam question would be "State and prove theorem number
14." The math book used for the ninth grade was first printed
in the 1880's. The students generally can't afford text books so
everything depends on the teacher. I will start my actual teaching after vacation. The present Agriculture teacher is leaving but
he will be replaced, I guess. I have a few ideas of things I want to
change around here, but most things are out of my control. Carl
and I have talked to the Principal of the College here about starting a math department. I read the syllabus for Logic and asked if I
could teach the Logic course. He said none of the students wanted
to take Logic, but if any do I can teach them. Here it's necessary
to teach everything in the syllabus no matter how worthless it is,
because the tests are given by the University and not the individual
teachers. In the college the students only take I.A. and B.A. exams
after two years each. Well, so much for that.

Our landlord is using the fact that we are Peace Corps people
living here to get the government to grant him permission to
install a water tap in the house. So they have been digging in the
basement and out to the water pipe in the street for the last three
days. Our house is on the main road to Banepa although the street
is less than fifteen feet wide. Whenever a truck or jeep would

Spectators at festival. (Mike Frame)

come by, they would have to quit working and lay some big timbers across the hole. The night before last, about ten o'clock, a big truck loaded with bags of rice and people broke one of the timbers and dropped one tire down in the hole. It took them about two hours to jack the thing up and get it out of there. It really raised a big crowd. They have pretty good plumbing equipment and do a job just like at home. Until now we have been going up the street and into a courtyard to stand in line with the ladies in order to get water. The people here have been wondering why we did it and didn't hire someone to do it. For one thing, here carrying water is women's work. Our cook wouldn't get water because of that.

There are all sorts of celebrations and festivals going on around here most of the time. They are in a way very informal but each has its own meaning and form which is in the tradition of hundreds of years. Just now a band of drums and cymbals went by, followed by a crowd of people. I asked Asteman (our cook) what it was but all he could tell me that I understood was *puja* (worship.) He doesn't speak any English except words like "lunch," "breakfast," "bread," "macaroni" and "pumpkin pie." He has taught me a lot of Nepali, especially vegetables' and spices' names. Lately he has been bringing his wife along to help him get supper. He doesn't have much imagination. Whenever we say we like something he makes it for the next three days. We have rice and *dal* (a kind of tiny bean in a sauce) at least once, sometimes twice a day. I am getting pretty used to it and my capacity has grown so that I can eat about three times as much rice now as I used to.

I just broke for supper—rice, *dal* and a kind of banana fritters. Now I'm listening to good old American popular music on Radio Ceylon. We get all the new songs and also the old favorites. I still haven't gotten to like Asian music too much. It still seems out of tune. But then I guess they feel the same way about our music.

Love, Mike

January 2, 1963
Kathmandu

Dear Mom and Dad,
I have about a hundred letters to write, so I guess I will write to you and then give up. I know that this gets read by quite a few people anyway.

Well, the holidays are over now and I can stand to lose a

little weight. Yesterday we went to one of the embassy secretary's for lunch, which turned out to be sort of a smorgasbord in the backyard for about a hundred or so people. Most of the brass in Kathmandu (except the King) were there. I knew about a dozen people, but that just gave me more time to eat rather than make small talk with all the people. Anyway there was plenty of good food and I kept up the Peace Corps reputation for eating plenty. We have gotten this reputation after several U.S.A.I.D. hostesses have run out of food or near it when P.C. people went to dinner at their homes. They don't realize how big our stomachs get when we eat rice for every meal. Thank goodness the holiday season is over, now we can settle down and do a few things. It was about the busiest Christmas I have ever spent. By the way, I kind of joined the church choir here; I sang in the Christmas Eve service, but I haven't made it to church on Sunday yet—always at school. It was really nice to see everyone again for a few days. Some of them had to walk two days to reach transportation, but they all came in. [We got] a little surface freight, our blankets, packs and tool kits, but my trunk hasn't come yet. By the way, A.P.O. is still coming; I could use an old egg beater and a good ear of corn. (They don't have any dent corn over here, only flint.)

Last Saturday Bob and I went out to Bhaktapur on our bicycles. He wanted to get some pictures and I wanted to see some of my friends. We had a pretty nice trip. We walked all over Bhaktapur; I knew of some out-of-the-way temples which are off the tourist routes so I showed them to Bob and then we got off on some streets I hadn't been on before and got into semi-private courtyards, and had a good time. In one of these a man called to us out of an upstairs window and came running down to show us a Tibetan prayer tapestry. It was really beautiful, but he wanted 400 rupees for it. We had to tell him that we didn't have very much money. I may go back sometime and try to get it for 200. These kinds of things came out with the refugees and may turn up most anywhere, but this was the best I have seen. Then we wandered back to the house. On the way I was greatly pleased to see a man feeding some weaning pigs. Before this I hadn't seen pigs eat anything but dung and garbage. I went over and tried to find out what he was feeding them but he didn't speak Nepali, and I couldn't tell by smell. I went to the house and talked to Luxmi and one of his brothers.

This Friday and Saturday we are planning a trip up to Kakani where we will get a good view of the Himalayas. It should be fun.

January 6

We had a pretty good time up at Kakani. We went with the landlord and the cast of the movie he is producing. One of the Peace Corps girls has a movie camera so he invited us so that he would have a camara. We rode most of the way up in a truck but had to go the last mile or two on foot. We took along a sack of rice, some bread, 20 chickens (alive) and a couple baskets of vegetables. The mountains were really terrific. When we woke up in the morning after a frosty night (half-inch deep frost) the valleys were filled with fog but the mountains were sticking up all over. The Himalayas were really beautiful. Mount Everest was barely visible in the far East. In the sunshine it got really hot although on the north slope the frost stayed almost all day. It was kind of fun being with all the actors. In the evening we sat around singing with them.

One guy came in stone drunk and stated the words perfectly of "Oh God our help in ages past, our hope for years to come." He said three verses of it and we just about died laughing the whole time. He didn't even sound like a Nepali—he could have just left any American bar. We had our cook with us and he got food and went with us to our friend's house up there and cooked. One of the P.C. boys is stationed up there on an experimental fruit farm. We then walked back yesterday afternoon. It took us about three hours of down-hill walking.

Love, Mike

January 7, 1963
Kathmandu

Last night I went to hear our assistant Peace Corps Representative [Willi Unseold] speak on his forthcoming Everest expedition. He will be the climbing leader of the party and is the only one of them now in Nepal. I guess the rest will be arriving daily from now on. It sounds like a pretty big expedition. They have 25 tons of food and equipment on its way and will have to hire nine hundred porters to carry it up to base camp. They will leave on February 20 from Banepa, which is just beyond Bhaktapur, so we will have a lot of traffic past our house before they start. When they get to base camp, after about three weeks trekking, they will hire about four hundred Sherpas (people who wear coats and boots) and let the nine hundred barefoot porters go back. They hope they don't hit too much snow with the barefoot ones, but he said that on the last Himalayan expedition he took, they walked barefoot in snow for three days without much trouble.

By the way, I got the pamphlets the other day and some look quite useful. I am also receiving the Dairy Goat Journal. If nothing else, it would be nice to leave a fair library of Ag. Books and pamphlets at the school when I leave. I hope I get the package you sent to Bhaktapur sometime. By the way, Mom, how about pancakes and baking powder biscuits? We're going to make an oven out of bricks and kerosene tins as soon as we get out to Bhaktapur next week.

January 14, 1963
Kathmandu

Today I rode out to Bhaktapur on my bike, since we had a holiday at the college. It was nice to get out there again and see all my friends. Luxmi told me that one of his friends said I could have the garden in his yard to plant, so we went there and looked it over. It seems pretty big considering I would have to dig it all by hand. I told him I would like part of it. If you could find some sweet corn seed that isn't hybrid it would really be great over here. . . . Almost all the corn here is eaten by humans in one way or another, and sweet corn might be a lot better since it can be dried or eaten fresh, when the stalks still have some nutrition in them for the cows. I don't want hybrid seed because it doesn't work well to save seed from hybrid plants. I would also like to try out some parsnips next winter. Any seeds you might send would be welcomed.

Last Friday a girl and I were going to walk to Bimphedi, which is 70 miles by the road (Raj Path) and only 18 miles by trail. We got up at 5:00 and I went over to her house for breakfast. Then we headed out with our packs and sleeping bags and food, hoping to make it in one day. When we reached the edge of the valley where the path leaves the road (about 6 miles) we ran into the police who wanted to see our passports. We hadn't needed them inside the valley so of course we hadn't thought to bring them along. So the police gave us tea and said we couldn't go any further without our passports.

We then left the road and headed back on the winding paths across the fields. We came to a hill with wide stone walks leading up it. At the top there was a town, which had the houses on the rim of it all built together in a circle like a fortress. We walked up the hill since we had never seen anything quite like this before. It turned out to be the prettiest town I have seen in Nepal. We walked through an old gate in the outer ring and found ourselves up against another row of houses inside, without a gate. The houses were very old with wood carvings all over them and in front of each doorstep there was a carved stone, sometimes decorated with flowers, etc. The streets were all paved with evenly set cut rocks. All over town there were carved stone shrines, all the same, of a type I hadn't seen before. The thing that impressed me most was that the streets were spotlessly clean and there weren't any dogs or pigs or even cows roaming the streets. In the center of town we went through a gate into the yard of a huge temple. Here we found the center of life for the community. The children climb on the smaller shrines and play around; the tailor is sitting in the sun on

the steps of the temple working with his Singer sewing machine; the women are washing clothes or their hair by the well, or drying rice in the sunshine. Some people were going through their own ritual of worship and many people just loafing in the sunshine. From there we got a wonderful view of the mountains and of the valley, which was spread out at our feet. We met the children of the town who were very excited at our coming. The people were all Newari so we couldn't communicate very well with them in Nepali. We found out that the town is called Kirtipur, which I had heard of before. It was mostly built in the ninth century and is primarily Buddhist. The story is that the town held out against one of the invading kings (which it could well do,) [and later, when he did conquer it, most of the people had their ears cut off, because of their resistance.] We finally left Kirtipur, followed by about a dozen boys. I felt sort of like the Pied Piper, but I knew the boys were hoping for some *paisa* (money,) which we didn't give. . . . We finally got back [to Kathmandu] and were kind of happy that we didn't go all the way to Bimphedi since we were sore in various spots and pretty tired. We are getting a little out of shape just sitting around and riding our bikes from time to time.

Saturday I slept and sat in the sun most of the morning and then went to the barber shop and had a shave and a haircut for a rupee. If I was Nepali I could get it for 75 paisa (6 bits) but blond hair is slightly harder to cut, you know; anyway it's pretty cheap, just 2/5 the price of this letter.

I will have to start getting down to work now for this workshop I'm attending. Until now I've been more or less a student, but next week I will have to start teaching. I am supposed to cover

Scene in Kirtipur. (Mary Ellen Frame)

the growing of wheat, oats, barley and sorghum for the agronomy class. It should be quite an experience—thank god someone else is doing rice. . . .

Love, Mike

January 23, 1963
Kathmandu

. . .Now I'm doing a little teaching at the teachers' workshop. We're planning an agronomy course. These men haven't studied agriculture before, so we are trying to wind them up for eight weeks so that they can unwind in their schools all year long. The Nepali teacher has been teaching them a few things about raising pasture crops but the class thought maintaining pastures was out of place in Nepal. I got up and told them what a good cow can produce and some facts about my father's farm and the price of milk and a few other things. They came to realize a few things although I wasn't in complete agreement with the Nepali instructor. The price of milk over here is slightly higher than it is at home, and considering everything else here costs one fifth to one tenth as much; the income from one cow on an acre of land would be pretty good if the cow would produce like yours. Here there are no health regulations about how the milk is taken care of so he could get along with just one or two old pails for equipment. The sale is directly to the consumer. But if many farmers tried this they would soon find themselves spending more for rice and getting less for their milk. Land is scarce and all of it is needed for rice production if the people are going to have a subsistence diet. By the way, land is priced here at about 1500 rupees per *ropani* (⅛ acre) and since there are 7.6 rupees per dollar official exchange rate, the land is about $1600 per acre. (On the black market you can get ten rupees for each dollar.) The government is trying to get the price of land down but with little success. When they buy land for a road or something they pay only 1000 rupees. The going interest rate here is 15% but this must be covered in gold. You can see why not many farmers own their own land. Most farm on half shares. The landlord may provide an irrigation canal, that's all.

Yesterday we went on a field trip to the Agriculture Department at Singha Durbar (means Lion Palace.) This is a huge rambling palace where the whole government bureaucracy is held. The place is really quite beautiful with many secondary buildings and a lot of grounds. Most of the land there, which was probably rose gardens in former times, is now in vegetables and crops. They are doing a wonderful job in trying new varieties and testing and raising seed. This is one of four such experimental farms in the country. They also had a pretty varied assortment of dairy cows over there. They had one big red cow there with foot-long horns, who reminded me of Gracie. She was by far the best looking cow I've seen since I've been here. I think the buffaloes here have far greater potential for development as dairy animals. In them it is possible to do a lot of selective breeding, which I think has been done in the past, since Nepalis eat the male animals. Many buffalo cows have very good udders and give more and higher butterfat milk than the cows. As for breeding cows, I think they are just let to run with the bulls in the street when they are in heat. They eat mostly rice straw and a protein compound made out of rice millings, and of course what grass grows along the roads and out of the foundations of temples.

There are quite a few Tibetans around town these days. I don't know whether they are refugees or if they have just come to trade. Many probably actually live in Nepal in the high mountains. They are generally bigger than the Nepali people. They all wear boots and heavy coats and they seem very happy, friendly and wildly full of fun. The Nepali people here are often barefoot even in freezing temperatures. The Tibetans are very colorful, often driving a flock of sheep and carrying huge loads on their backs, although I have seen them with ponies, which stand about waist-high and carry packs. They have brought along rumors of the Chinese massing just behind that beautiful white ridge. Some people expect them in April or May when the passes open up. Don't worry about me, Mom. I can make it out the front door far faster than they can come in the back. No more than three days, even if I have to go on foot, but they can't get from the north in less than ten.

The new Agriculture teacher who is coming to Bhaktapur to help me is from the far West. When he came he had to walk for eleven days out the west side of Nepal to a place in India where he got a train and came around, then up the Raj Path by bus. I would sure like to go back there with him some time. One of my big jobs here is to try to help the other teachers in addition to teaching the students. I want to leave a good Ag. department in Bhaktapur when I leave. But I can do this best through example, doing a good job teaching the students there now. By the way, I

Tibetans selling rugs. (Mike Frame)

can use any kind of vegetable seed—tomato, carrot, head lettuce, PEAS, asparagus, melon squash, SWEET CORN, beet, potato eyes, parsnip, or anything else—nothing hybrid. I'm going to try and get a couple of strawberry plants from the mission in Banepa. Now that I have my own garden I can go to work. I will try to use their tools but it will be kind of hard on this hard clay soil. I can eat lettuce without danger if I grow it myself.

February 4, 1963
Bhaktapur

Dear Bill and Sandy,
I kind of wish we would get a little snow here. It gets down below freezing at night but always warms up to about seventy in the daytime. The problem is that the houses don't have any way to be heated and the only way to get away from the cold is to go to bed, but then it's real cold in the morning.

Yesterday we got back from a five-day trip to the South. The biggest thing about the trip was the Raj Path. It is seventy-two miles of the roughest road in the world. There are seventeen hundred turns in it and the whole thing is up and down in low gear. It was really beautiful. We would meet big trucks sometimes when we went around a corner and would have to back up until we found a place wide enough to pass. It takes six or seven hours to drive it. A trail which goes to the same place is only eighteen miles and takes about ten hours [walking.] By a straight line it's ten or twelve miles. There wasn't a piece of straight road more than fifty

Terraced hillsides. (Mike Frame)

yards long in the whole trip. We climbed out of the valley up to
about six thousand, five hundred feet, then we dropped down to
about four thousand, then up to over seven thousand and down
to five hundred. On the way back there was a tremendous view of
the great white mountains in the north. From far in the east to far
in the west there was a ridge of white. Coming up this road, built
by Indian engineers and American money and lots of Nepali hand
labor, we could see the biggest problem Nepal is facing. There just
isn't any easy way of transportation in this country. We had quite
a trip with all the Nepali school teachers in school busses. We ate
at tea shops along the road and spoke a lot of Nepali and really
got to know some of them quite well. About three of them threw

up on the way down because the road was so rough but on the way back they took it pretty well.

It's really different down there from here. We went to the Rapti valley, which was all jungle until a couple of years ago and was so infested with malaria that hardly anyone lived there. Now it's really booming. We found darker people there, the Tharus, who have always been in the jungle and have built up a slight immunity to malaria, and the bigger people who look like Indians. They have almost gotten rid of malaria. They have cleared hundreds of acres of jungle and are having people settle the land and farm it. They have made the purchasing pretty easy and have put a limit [on what each family can buy] so that they wouldn't end up with a lot of rich landowners like in the rest of Nepal. The area was really fantastic. It made me think of the frontier prairie settlement, which was going on a hundred years ago [in America.] There is a big Ag. Experiment station there where they are growing everything from pineapples to alfalfa. There the houses are all made out of wood and are so constructed that they will keep out the rain and tigers. Many of them are built on stilts with thatched roofs and rough-hewn logs. There were oxcarts along the roads and really not too many people around. We rode through part of the less dense jungle and it was very nice. All I could hear when we stopped were strange bird sounds. There were many strange birds and trees. It was quite a ride going down through the valley. We had to ford streams quite often and it was pretty rough gravel all the way. In many places they don't really build bridges, instead they build a cement structure with a few culverts in it which goes fairly low over the water. When the monsoon comes the water will just pour over but it won't be washed out. When the rains aren't too bad it can be forded. Wherever they had regular bridges instead of these they were usually washed out and we had to ford the streams.

We also went down to Birgunj, which is right on the border of India and really quite similar [to India.] There were many rickshas, horse-drawn carts, oxcarts, trucks and we even saw an elephant being ridden down the street. It was a very busy town. There we stayed with a couple of Peace Corps boys who lived there and three other PCVs who were passing through, so we had a pretty good time. We had quite a trip with all the Nepali school teachers in school busses. Usually I slept with Americans, but one night I stayed with the Nepali teachers, that we got well acquainted with. Of course this was quite an experience for them. They all looked over my sleeping bag, and watched me undress, asking if Americans sleep naked and all sorts of irregular questions. We sat around and sang songs and played some Nepali card games (which are really screwed up.) On the trip we ate most of the time in small tea houses where the food wasn't too bad and we got rather adept at eating with our fingers, which is quite a skill. The Nepalis use only the right hand for eating, the other being reserved for other things, since they don't use toilet paper. If you were to use your left hand for eating, they would think you were terribly unclean, like picking your nose in church.

Love, Mike

February 21, 1963
Bhaktapur

Bhaktapur is a going place these days. It's the wedding season so the bands and processions are going by all night. I can hear one coming right now; it sounds like a couple of un-tuned bagpipes (but they are flutes,) a couple drums and cymbals. The bride is carried in a chair with a pole in front and back carried by two men. They are usually dressed pretty fancily. I can't make very many generalizations about the marriage customs since each family or sub-caste has its own and they are sometimes quite different.

One festival is going on daily here around town; it is for the Goddess of fishermen. It is celebrated each day in a different neighborhood or *tole* by one of the farmer sub-castes. Anyway there are half a dozen beggars connected to it, dressed in bright red costumes with mountains of jewelry and masks. It is the custom to give them a few *paisa,* so I've been hit pretty hard since they've been in three places on my way to school already. The evening when it was in our *tole* I watched quite a bit of it. The Fisherman God, with a big white mask on, runs after the little children (the fish) and when he catches them he tickles them. Later on he cuts a baby pig open with his fingernail and takes out the heart while it is still beating. It is quite a festival. Many of the people were a little drunk.

There are many Indians in town now. They have come on a pilgrimage to one of our temples. They look quite strange with their sacks of possessions placed haphazardly on their heads. They walk all over and never pay any attention to what they are carrying. Otherwise things are pretty quiet around here except for a man who goes by chanting, every morning about four o'clock. One morning I didn't hear him, but the next morning he went by at 3:30 and then again at 4:30. I guess he had to make up for sleeping in the morning before.

The day before yesterday after school, I went on a walk with Luxmi over to see the garden which I will plant soon. It won't be too terribly far to carry water for irrigation, but that will be the biggest problem. After we looked it over we walked to part of the town where I hadn't been before and then went out into the country. There was a spring-like fresh breeze out there, and the air smelled so good that it made me a little homesick. It reminded me of the times in the spring at home when the snow had melted and the ground had just dried off enough in the pasture to lie down on it, but there would still be water running in the valleys. It was just like that there; the trees were bare; the fields were brown except for fields of green wheat where there was irrigation water available.

We saw where they were digging coal out of the ground so we walked over there. It's a real poor grade of coal, which was only about five feet under the surface. They use this only to fire their bricks, since it smells too bad to use in the house. Not far from there, down the hill a little, we found some farmers digging for *kali mati*, a black clay used for fertilizer. Here they had dug a hole about a yard in diameter, going at an angle into the ground so that they could cut out high steps on the bottom side. These go down about fifty feet to reach the fertilizer. At one time the entire Kathmandu Valley was a lake bed, so these rich deposits were laid down in some places to a very great depth. These pits are pretty dangerous; last year three men died in one near here.

We then came back to the potters' *tole*. There we saw hundreds of the shallow dishes, which are used for curd, being dried all over the place. We watched one man making these. He started with a great big pile of clay on the middle of his wheel; he got the great big wheel going really fast by using a stick which he stuck in a hole by the edge. The wheel did not rotate on the level, but the portion in the middle was level where he put his clay. He could shape one of these dishes in about half a minute, tossing in a little water here and there to ease friction and cutting it off with a piece of string. For some reason he made them all bottomless; we watched another man putting bottoms in when they were almost dry. Anyway, he could get eight or ten dishes from one piece of clay and a good spin. They bake these by piling them up with straw and covering the pile over with mud with holes in it, and set fire to it. . . .

Love, Mike

March 31, 1963
Shri Padma High School, Bhaktapur

I seem to be getting busier and busier and at the same time doing less and less. Yesterday being Saturday, I went to the garden fairly early (9:00) and worked up a fair sized piece of ground. I used the local tool, *kodali* to plow up the land. It's a back-breaker, but it sure is a lot faster than a spade, and it turns the soil better. I came home about 10:00 and got a little to eat and drink and then I took my hoe and seed over, hoed it all twice, and planted sweet

Potter at his wheel. (Mike Frame)

corn, squash, string beans and lettuce. I used the whole packages of beans and corn because if it grows well there are a number of people I would like to give it to and I should save some for seed. I've got some tomatoes planted in a flat on our roof and if I ever get my stiffness and blisters taken care of I'll plow up some more land. There were lots of people watching me. One farmer didn't particularly like the way I was using the *kodali* so he gave me a demonstration, and I tried to do it that way and found it was easier. You should never underestimate the skill of a laborer and expect to do as well when you start out. When I came back and started hoeing no one was around because it was lunch time for them, so I took off my shirt and ended up with a sunburn. When I started planting there was a whole crowd around. I don't think they thought much of the sweet corn since it was so small and shriveled. . . .

I'm at school now and sitting as usual with not much to do. I've taken over the tenth grade English Prose course now so I'm a little busier. One tenth grader comes fairly irregularly to be tutored before school in math, and one has come a couple times after school to learn English. He is a pretty good artist and we talk about his pictures quite a bit.

April 11, 1963   Happy New Year
Bhaktapur   Chaitre 29, 2019

We are having the biggest festival of the year here in Bhaktapur. They have put together a huge temple on a wagon called *Rath*. This has three roofs and rises to the height of a three-story building. The wheels are made out of beams about eight inches thick, and it is pulled by seven two-inch ropes on each end. They start in the Five Story Temple Square where they have been assembling it for weeks and have been making replacement parts.

Then, about seven last night, the men from the *tallo* bazaar (bottom or lower bazaar) were pulling toward the south west end of town and the people from *maathi* bazaar (top or upper bazaar) were pulling toward the north east. Just as they were getting started it started raining so we all took cover and got back after the cart had left the square. This thing is fantastically heavy and hard to manage since it rides on two fixed axles. They have a man riding on each end coaxing all the people on that side to pull and it really rocks back and forth in a tug of war. He shouts something like "Hoo-say;" the others shout "Eee-say." "Hoo-say!" "Eee-say!" "Ah, ah, ah, ah, ah" as they pull together. When both sides chant the same the wagon just shakes; but when they chant and pull alternately, it rocks back and forth. They shut off all the electricity in town because no one is sure where the temple will be going, but they take the wires down where it is sure to go. When we got back after the rain, after a couple of chess games in candle light (I'm learning how to watch the game intelligently, but haven't tried playing yet,) the temple had been pulled way down in *tallo* bazaar and one wheel had sunk into the ground a couple of feet at the side of the road and the top was up against the eaves of a house. A man was carried by, who had been side-swiped by a wheel. Then it started to rain again. I went with Budri to his home, which is near there and talked to him for an hour or so. He is about my best friend here. After the rain we went back again and they were trying to jack up the temple with some long beams and then they tried to pull it again but there weren't enough people. Usually they would do this all night long, but last night the rain sort of put a damper on it. I finally got home about midnight, after having tea and a boiled egg in a tea shop. This morning I was awakened about eight when Budri and another friend came and told me that they were moving the carriage again. When we got to it, it was up against a wall and they were having a hell of a time steering it. It is to rest in a valley for two days now. When they got it away from the wall and started it down the hill, I didn't think anything was going to stop it. But it came to rest without killing

Rath festival. (Mike Frame)

Rath festival. (Mike Frame)

Rath festival. (Mike Frame)

anyone. Then the children pulled another, smaller temple on wheels from the square down into the hollow with the big one. This was done without major incident but it was lots of fun. . . .

June 25, 1963
Bhaktapur

I guess the monsoon has hit now but it isn't really too bad. It doesn't rain more than five or six times a day. Yesterday it was nice almost all day and three of my friends came out from Kathmandu and wanted a tour of Bhaktapur, so we started out walking. I asked them if they wanted to see what *they* wanted to see (i.e. only the main tourist attractions,) or what I wanted to show them. We met my friend Budri along the way and I told him to come along and tell them the names of all the temples and the stories of the gods. So we took a grand tour and went way down to the north-east end of town, showed them a few temples there and then watched the potters there for a while. It's just amazing how they can form things so quickly and well out of clay on their big wheels. Then there was a temple about half a mile outside of town which Budri wanted to show them, so we walked out there. On the way back we hit a few out-of-the-way temples which tourists never see, my garden (which tourists never see,) one Buddha and a really interesting Buddhist temple which is in a back alley. Julie Goetze said she hadn't seen any pornography, so I took her to see the temple in the square that has figures on it in all the positions of intercourse. When she saw it she felt too shy to walk

Rice planting. (Mike Frame)

around and look at it. We walked way down to the south-west end of town and back through the main square with the five-story temple (which you have pictures of.) They came back [to my house] and had lunch with us and then left for Kathmandu on their bicycles just before we got an awful rain, the hardest I've seen so far. The street in front of our house turned into a roaring stream about six inches deep, since our house is about half way down a hill. I haven't seen my garden since then, but the corn in the school garden is all knocked down.

Now they are busy transplanting rice out in the fields. I'm getting a few squash and cucumbers from my garden now. . . .

August 2, 1963
Bhaktapur

. . . Carl came home from Kathmandu last Monday and said that
the Peace Corps Representative wanted to send an Agriculture
teacher to Dhankuta because the teacher's wife there had gotten
pregnant and they are going home, and that I was one of the three
boys on his mind. Because of this I didn't go in the next day as
I had planned, but waited a day to let the representative know
that I wasn't anxious. I went in on Wednesday morning . . . to
the Peace Corps building and fooled around most of the day and
finally met the Representative in the hallway and got urgently
invited into his office. They are sending one person out there for
six weeks and then it might be me after that. (Probably.) I didn't
say "no" and I didn't say "yes." I guess that probably means yes.
But I have six weeks to clean things up here now. The deal is,
they got a sow and a boar out there from the government farm,
(Hampshire, I think) and they don't have anyone out there who
knows how to take care of them. He also had three classes of
Agriculture, a garden and some chickens that aren't doing very
well. Since I'm not doing anything very much here, they think
it's a good chance for me to do something and they really need
someone to go out there. I don't really mind going to a place that
is a day's walk from the nearest "road" where there isn't electricity and only a market once a week, but I do kind of mind leaving
Bhaktapur without really getting anything accomplished. I find it
kind of hard to leave the people here. . . . Otherwise I'd still just
as soon get out of this school here since it is multi-purpose and

government-run. I guess I'll just be inactive and get put where somebody wants me. . . .

As far as I can remember, the last time a Minnesota boy went over the trail between Dharan and Dhankuta, he fell seventy feet and landed in a hospital in Duluth—but don't worry, Mom, people are also eaten by tigers.

August 6, 1963
Bhaktapur

Dear William and Sandy,

. . . Today is one of the biggest festivals of the year here, and right now I am taking a little break from it. There is one route that goes around most of the town and is about two or three miles long. This morning the people who had a relative die during the year have a thing with horns on top to represent a cow and then they carry this the whole way around town with dancers and drums and all sorts of noise. The costumes of the dancers have a pretty wide range: everything from little boys with nothing on except dabs of cotton all over their bodies to people with complete coats of hair, or grass skirts, or men dressed as women. They all carried sticks or tools and each pair of people knocked them together with the beat of the drums.

August 7

I didn't get too far on this letter yesterday. Budri asked me over to his house for the feast yesterday afternoon. His mother and aunt had already eaten before we got there, so just the two of us ate together. We had a special kind of broth made out of all kinds of pulses, peas and beans which was pretty good. Then we had fried brown flat bread, then corn (their local corn tastes like overripe sweet corn,) lots of buffalo meat and some hot curried vegetables. I really ate quite a bit of this stuff and it all tasted pretty good. Either I'm getting used to this kind of food or this was better than I've had at other things like this, but I'm liking it better. After eating, we toured the town in the opposite direction to how the bands and dancers were going so that we could see almost everything. Some had made clay cows, which they carried; others led real cows along, which they would give to a Brahmin afterward; only the rich can afford to give away cows. Anyway we got caught in the rain and had to sit in a shelter for an hour. Some of the dancers went right on, rain or no rain. I spent the evening sitting in a boot store in the Bazaar and then I went to one boy's room over a shop where we could watch the dancers at will when they came along, and we spent the rest of the time sitting around talking. There were mostly Budri's friends there including two that I teach English to every morning. We spoke in English most of the time and it was fairly enjoyable for me for a change since usually when I'm with a group of these people, they all speak Newari that I don't understand at all.

I'm back in school today. I taught my English class of three students and now I don't have much to do for a while. The attendance is pretty bad here since the students only have to come to class 75% of the days. Even then they might leave before my period. We are teaching English in the sixth grade now, after dividing them into classes of about 15 students. We are using mostly an oral approach and quite different methods than have been used here before.

Love, Mike

August 13, 1963
Bhaktapur

. . . Last Saturday there was a party for our Peace Corps Representative who is going home this week. We had a good time and Mrs. Unseold put on a tremendous feed. You might remember Willi Unseold, our assistant representative, was one of the men who climbed Mt. Everest last spring. We had a good time listening to his tales, while we sat and looked at his feet. His toes are all black and the bases of them are all raw. He will lose parts of all his toes except one little one. He was complaining about having to keep one toenail trimmed. Well, I guess he was lucky only to lose a few toes on that mountain. He will be the representative now as soon as he can come back to work.

Mike, Mac Odell, and Gokul Man Shrestha (headmaster) in Dhankuta. (Mickey Veich)

Dhankuta, 1963–64

LETTERS

September 17, 1963
Mathillo Kopche
Dhankuta, Nepal
P.O. Jogbani, Dist. Purnea
Via India

Dear Mom and Dad,
In a couple of days I will have been here a week. . . . Everything came off alright in my travels, except that I didn't have any time, as I had planned, to stop and see anyone. We flew to Biratnagar on Wednesday and traveled the thirty miles to Dharan by bus. There is a gradual increase in altitude between Biratnagar and Dharan, which is right at the base of the mountains. Biratnagar is really flat and just like an Indian town anywhere on the plains of India. In Dharan there is a British recruiting camp for Gurkha soldiers, so we rode on a British-built road, which was very nice and we could see the mountains getting closer and closer which was really welcome, since the heat on the plain was stifling. We stayed at the Peace Corps house in Dharan. Harold Christianson lives there. From his porch we could see across the

strip of jungle along the base of the mountains and look out over the plains of India and just barely see the wide Ganges on the western horizon.

Thursday we had a slightly contrasting experience traveling [steep ups and downs, on foot] which took just twelve hours, including many tea stops, and a two-hour stop for lunch. We got here about seven in the evening. I only brought a little stuff with me that day, the rest of it came a few days later on the back of a porter.

Things are a bit different here, no friends yet. The people mostly speak Nepali, although the merchant class here is also Newari. The others are Rais and Limbus, who have their own languages. The teachers at school speak better English than those in Bhaktapur and seem pretty on the ball. However, the school is pretty hard to teach in, since the walls between the classrooms are just boards with wide cracks between them and some doors and windows. I have a double period each day in Agriculture: two days seventh, two days sixth and one day eighth grades.

September 20

Yesterday was Bazaar day so we had a holiday from school. And we all went to market. All the people come in from the country-side around, with their baskets full of all sorts of things. We put in a week's supply of rice, bananas, potatoes, tomatoes, apples, limes, pineapples, ghee, peanuts, squash, corn (for the pigs,) cracked corn (for the chickens and us,) fish, meat, eggs, cucumbers, onions, ginger, garlic, baskets, mats and all sorts of nameless vegetables and fruits. In the afternoon we all went for a picnic to a stream about two hours away. There we went swimming, had sandwiches, apples, boiled eggs, cold liver and banana bread. We all had a real good time. There were six of us, the Hambricks, who live separately, Mac Odell and Barb Wylie, with whom I live, and our cook, Boody. It was dark on the way home so we stopped to see an Indian Major and his wife who live at the upper end of town. He works giving out pension money to the [retired] Gurkha soldiers here. The major's wife had borrowed my flashlight. He brought out beer and some orange drink for Barb and me and some food. Then we played bridge for about an hour or so. It was really a nice rest before we came the rest of the way home.

. . . I've found that I really don't like to teach school very well; I would rather just stick around here and work with the garden, the pigs and the chickens. I also enjoy cooking here since we have a real nice kitchen. I've been trying different ways with pancakes with your recipe, Mom. I've been using curds, sour milk and whey and having great results. I'm sort of in charge of getting the breakfast around here. We have a cook who always is doing the supper dishes at that time and I'm lucky if I can get him to bring in some firewood and start the fire.

Everything here is just up and down; no car could ever make it up most of these streets even if they could get into the town. I am liable to get in shape just by going to school every day. Down by the school, though, there is a flat piece of ground about as big as our front lawn, which the Rana government had made once for a playing field.

I'm going to get up early tomorrow and start digging the garden, although the fence still doesn't keep out the chickens. I'm not very good at weaving bamboo and branches. Still don't have the sow bred. I put them [sow and boar] in separate pens so they would quit feeling so much like brother and sister. I think we will get another sow pretty soon and use the boar some more on the local sows that are really pitiful. Must close now. Hope you are all well.

Love, Mike

September 30, 1963
Dhankuta

. . . The last couple of days a friend of Barbara's from Kathmandu was here, but he has gone now. It was sort of a wild time for all of us to have a visitor around here. He went to school with Mac and me and we let it appear that he was as much or more our friend as Barbara's. This is a really conservative town (not quite as bad as Bhaktapur perhaps) so when he came Barb told him not to touch her. I'm afraid they didn't get much time alone together. He has sent us quite a bit of food from the American commissary where the A.I.D. people get their food. Although Barb is a vegetarian, he has also sent us some things with meat in them.

It rained for two or three days but it got over with it yesterday. A man came and wanted some work so I put him to work on my garden fence which I couldn't seem to build so it would hold out the chickens. It's going to take him three days and it only took me about three hours. I guess that's the difference. Anyway, I finished plowing the garden up and put some ashes, chicken and pig dung on it. Dung is all we seem to be getting out of the chickens and

Market day. (Mary Ellen Frame)

pigs these days. The sow still isn't pregnant and I don't know what to do. I'm growing a garden here if it's the last thing I do. I might start planting tomorrow.

I've quit teaching Ag. at the high school since I decided it was pretty senseless. It is hard to teach anything new in a practical manner as they want. The farmers here have been using fairly correct methods for a thousand years and if we take the students into a garden we end up teaching ninety percent of the time the same methods. I would like to teach them a little of the science of agriculture, but this gets fairly difficult. I can say anything I want to say in Nepali now, but I use the same words over and over again. This means that the class has to be interested or they lose hold of what I'm getting at. The boys here just aren't interested and they

aren't used to my way of saying things either. So I have joined
my boys up with Mac and his carpentry class and we are going to
build an addition onto the school and some badly needed parti-
tions in between the classrooms. We have the bricks and the wood
and there isn't much else needed except a driving force to get the
work done. Our head master is really a hard worker and the other
teachers are enthusiastic—slightly different from the lazy group
in Bhaktapur who would go to their classes when there were ten
minutes left in the period. This, I think is a much better school
although the building is pretty bad.

Last Saturday, Mac, Mimi and I went up (when we say "up"
or "down" here, we really mean it—in this case about a thousand feet up, perhaps a half a mile away) to the major's where
Mimi and I were invited for lunch and an afternoon of bridge.
Mac went along so Barb and Jim could be alone. The Indian
Cultural Attaché to Nepal was staying with the major while
inspecting the area, so we ate with him also. He was all tired of
literary meetings, so he didn't do much but complain. The major
is thinking of starting a social club where people could go one
night a week and play games or have discussions, since there
just isn't anything to do here in the evening and there are a lot
of intellectual type people here. Must close now. Just think, I've
been in Nepal a whole year now.

Love, Mike

October 2, 1963
Dhankuta

. . . I'm sort of enjoying the new experience of living in the hills where there isn't quite the contact with the outside world. So what if many of the people here haven't seen an automobile or bicycle. The children don't know what a wheel is; they know what a helicopter is. I'm still not living in a thatched hut or anything, but you might be impressed by our cow-dung floors. Actually, it's quite good. Each week our cook goes out and collects a handful off the street and brings it in, mixes it with red clay and perhaps a little lime and water and washes down all our floors with it. We call it our new linoleum; it's really quite hard and clean. We don't use chairs here but we have nice bamboo stools and plenty of mats and pads on the floor for sitting and lying on.

One thing here is that food is really cheap and we really eat well. Tonight for supper we had a pork roast cooked with pineapple, potatoes with butter, squash, *dal* (lentils with onions,) a fruit salad--pineapple, bananas, guavas and *naspatis* (cross between apple and pear—large, three for a penny) and lime juice to drink. For breakfast we usually have pancakes or boiled, cracked corn (like oatmeal) and *naspati* sauce. . . .

October 10, 1963
Dhankuta

Here it's market day again and I guess it's time to send a note home. Today was the biggest market we've had since I've been here and I really had a good time buying things. It's sort of a game we play, running around looking for things and haggling over the price. One of the difficulties I found at first was the prevalence of Indian money here. Everything is quoted in *annas*, which are one sixteenth of an Indian rupee. So when the woman says she will give me two *naspatis* for an anna, I say three and end up buying five for two *annas*. The trouble is there are no *anna* coins anymore so we use different combinations of coins to make an *anna*. If you have Nepali money, however, it is quite simple, since ten Nepali *paisa* is exactly equal to one *anna*. If a *seer* of meat costs *ek rupya barra anna,* that comes to sixteen *annas* plus twelve *annas* or two rupees, eighty *paisa* in Nepali. (An *anna* is roughly equal to one and a fourth cents). Another thing you have to think about is the availability of different things. Last week only one man in the whole market had any limes and there weren't any lemons. Today, early in the morning, he called to me to sell me the few limes that he had, which were sort of puny, but the price was eight for one *anna*. I bought these quick because I didn't think I would find any more. Later I met the cook who had bought a whole rupee's worth of real nice lemons. Later on there were all kinds of limes and lemons. Almost the same thing happened with pineapples. The bananas got steadily cheaper as the day went on and the *naspati*, which are going out of season got steadily more expensive.

Walnuts (English walnuts, but harder to crack than black walnuts, Dad) are coming in now and so are tangerines and oranges. As you see, things are pretty cheap here. I spent a couple of hours there haggling and brought my shopping bag home four or five times to empty it and I couldn't have spent over fifty cents. The market is sort of like a department store. The butcher has a couple of buffalo and five or six pigs in one place. The lane going to one part of town has mostly shoes, *khukuri* knives and leather goods. Then there is a row of men selling ginger roots and garlic with little piles spread out on a cloth, each pile for one anna. Dried fish and onions are sold by the same people in another place, probably because they smell so bad. The townspeople take over the main drag where they set up tents with cloth, jewelry and odds and ends like soap and wax and spices. There is a place for sugar, a place for tobacco, a place for *ghee* (clarified butter) which comes in wooden pots, a place for rice, peanuts and Tibetan blankets. Vegetables and fruits are all over. There are also things like honey, which are only available occasionally.

We have one more week of school now before the two-week Desain festival. Right now in school we are having the school annual function where they have debates, sports, essay competition, art, cultural show and all sorts of things. It will last three or four more days. After Desain the final exams will start quite soon, so our school year is actually almost finished, although there is a month and a half left. I don't know what I'm going to do during Desain yet. It all depends on my friends. Budri might be coming out then and we would go on a trek or perhaps go to Darjeeling in India. Otherwise I will sort of stick around here, perhaps take

the boar on a trek and have him sow a few seeds in the villages. On market day, all sorts of villagers come here to look at the pigs but it's too far for them to bring their sows.

October 11
Guess what! The sow came in heat this morning. The boar gets interested once in a while but he hasn't bred her yet. I'll keep my eye on them for a couple of days. I don't know how long the heat periods last, or how frequent they are, so I don't know when to expect it. . . .

The social life in Dhankuta is fairly rushing compared to Bhaktapur. The only problem is that it is mostly Indians and Americans and not very many Nepalis. We have Indian army officials, Indian doctors and college professors who all speak excellent English. The night before last, we went to a cocktail party at the Major's where there was Scotch whiskey and Danish beer (lemonade for me.) Pretty cosmopolitan for being a day's walk from a road.

Love, Mike

November 4, 1963
Dhankuta

Dear Folks,
Help! Quick! We don't have a dressing recipe for stuffing! We've invited all sorts of people out here for Thanksgiving—perhaps thirty—and we don't have a recipe for the dressing for the ducks.

We are having a hard time getting sage but it will probably be found somewhere. We're also missing cranberry sauce, but we have just about everything else lined up including mincemeat and pumpkin pie.

They thank you for your lemon pudding recipe, Mom. We had it tonight and my friends thought it was great.

Since I last wrote to you, all sorts of things have happened. A week ago Friday night, Budri and I left for Dharan. We swam in a stream and took our time and found a place to sleep for the night. We ordered our rice and *dal* and were just ready to eat when Ralph showed up alone—his wife was sick. He ate with us and then we found out the restaurant we were at only had one blanket to give us. They had all sorts of mats though which we piled up and Ralph had brought along his sleeping bag, so we, all three of us, slept on the blanket and under the sleeping bag laid out flat. Real cozy. The next morning we were in Dharan bright and early and Budri left for Kathmandu. I got a shave in a barbershop and then in the afternoon went to Hal's wedding. After the wedding supper we went to a new house, which is being built behind Hal's house. There was only a floor up on poles. There we played bridge most of the night with a flashlight hung from above. The next day, Ralph, Dave Sears and I went down to the farm on the edge of the jungle where Dave works. Then we caught a bus to Dubi (halfway to Biratnagar) where we looked up a man in order for him to find us some horses. Well, they brought the first horse, which was blind in one eye and weighed perhaps 300 pounds. We said, the others must be better and none of us wanted to take it. They weren't. The next one came lame and the last was even smaller than

Mike with children in Dhankuta. (Photographer unknown)

the other two. In spite of everything, we started out for Inerwal,
which is nine or ten miles west of there. It was quite a trip. We
crossed innumerable streams, and my horse didn't seem to want to
go where I told it to, so once it went in deeper than I thought it
should and I had to jump for the bank when it sank up to its ears
in mud. The gunny sack saddle wasn't too wet, so I got on again
after pulling the horse out. We rode on and came to a bridge made
out of a hollowed-out log. I got across just fine; Dave got three
quarters of the way across and his horse jumped for the opposite
bank; Ralph and his horse got half way across. We next saw Ralph
hanging from the bridge. We almost died laughing. The trip was so
ridiculous anyway on those little horses. We got to Inerwal about
dark and met the new volunteers living there . The next morning

we came back on foot, stopping at all the tea shops along the way. We got to Dubi at the same time the horses did.

This morning at school I met one of the Hindu wise men. He stopped in at school and knew everyone in town and in all the towns around. He spoke perfect English and at one time taught in this school. He was dressed in an orange cloth and carried a crooked stick and other things. He said he originally came from Madras in South India, but he has traveled all over Nepal. His talk was quite interesting since he would be gossiping about people and then pretty soon he would be spouting philosophy and quoting from Jesus Christ and saying that all Gods and religions are the same and that love is the most important thing. We will probably be seeing more of him the next couple of days. We often see these wise men traveling around but I never met one before that spoke English. Usually they don't speak much Nepali either, but some Indian language or Sanskrit. . . .

Love, Mike

November 12, 1963
Dhankuta

. . . The farming is going fairly well. The garden is looking better, with lots of people looking at it. The pigs are all right, except they were (I hope I can use past tense) getting out of the pen, and running all over town. The sow took it well (she may be pregnant!) but the boar had too much fun and didn't come back a couple of nights. Now he's back in the pen, but he's really gotten thin. I expect quite a few crossbreds in this town pretty soon for all his wear.

I'm watching the senior class examination but they aren't cheating too much so I'm not too busy. It's sort of getting cold around here a little bit now and I'm glad school will be out soon. We often take the classes outside in the sunshine where it is always warm enough for short sleeves.

When Barbara was in Kathmandu for our two-week vacation, she met a tourist sort of girl who was staying there for awhile. Well, Barb brought her back and she will be staying with us until after Thanksgiving. She's a big help around here and of course she's another person to talk with. Now that three new P.C.V.s have come, we have nine Americans in Dhankuta.

Last night Mimi made a chocolate cake for me and had us all over for my birthday party. We went over after our night school English class. It was a good cake and a good party, except we got on the subject of latrines and talked about them about half the evening. What a party! . . .

Two days ago we had a missionary stop in here on her way from her post in Okhaldunga—which is halfway between Kathmandu and Darjheeling. Sometimes we think we are way out of it, but if we got up really early in the morning (2:00 AM) and made connections just right, we could be in Kathmandu in the afternoon. Think of the people in Bojhpur, two days from here and the missionaries in Okhaldunga, seven days away. Anyway, this nurse ate supper with us and was surprised when we brought out corn fritters with syrup, squash with a tomato-onion sauce, and a green salad (from my garden.) She thought we ate awfully well from just what we got in the local market. She said they'd never thought of using the cracked corn, or making syrup from sugar. One thing I can say for this outfit is that Barbara is a vegetarian; she knows how to make a meal without meat and this makes all the difference. We are lucky if we get meat here more than once a week. They almost always butcher on market day, but otherwise no one knows when they will butcher. . . .

December 3, 1963
Dhankuta

Thanksgiving is finally over and the last of the guests left today. We had a really great time—quite a bit bigger celebration than I think we ever had at home. We started cooking about last Monday—banana breads, spice cakes, gingerbreads, cookies and pies. And I tell you we cooked. My oven is the latest great innovation. In the market we found heavy iron cooking pots, which were hemispherical in shape and about fifteen inches across. So I built a little fireplace behind the house to set the two pots on together. With a little fire under it, my little sphere looked somewhat like a satellite ready to go into orbit. I made a little rack to put inside it, which would hold two pies. The system was to get one hemisphere hot, flip it over so the hot one was on top, and put the food in. It worked like a charm. I had to keep chucking wood under it for three days. My job was the pies. I used the mincemeat, which I brought with me, put some dried *naspatis* (apple-pears) with it and also some soured *naspati* cider. It was really good. I made one mincemeat pie early to try it out, and two for the dinner. I also made two pumpkin pies, one *naspati*, one chocolate and a lemon pie which didn't set properly, so we ate it ourselves. They all turned out pretty well, even the meringue.

The night before Thanksgiving we had sort of a big party at the new volunteers' house to listen to the address by our new President [Lyndon Johnson.] What's going on in America anyway? We had tea and cookies with many of our interested Nepali friends and the few PCVs who had come by then.

Thanksgiving morning, when we were just ready to buy our neighbor's big rooster and kill the four chickens we had already bought, our friends from Bhojpur came in with a pea-hen they had bought. So instead of turkey we had pea-hen for Thanksgiving. We fried three of the chickens while I made dressing and roasted the pea-hen in my oven. While we were doing this, Mimi was cooking a big imported ham and Ralph, her husband, was cooking a ham they had bought in the market that very morning (Thursday is market day.) At my place, we made a green salad of young beets with greens and mustard greens, from my garden. At their house, Mimi and Ralph made candied sweet potatoes, a wonderful fruit salad and hors d'oeuvres. The new fellows made punch, a big tub full of onion soup, and a mound of potatoes. They also prepared their house for the feast, and served the food. Altogether there were about twenty-five of us. And feast we did. There really weren't too many things left over. After the meal we waited a couple of hours before having dessert, so my pies were almost entirely eaten. They especially went for the pumpkin pies, one of which was baked in a pan twelve inches in diameter. The pea-hen and the dressing I made also came out wonderful—much better than turkey.

The day after Thanksgiving we all went to the school playing field—the only place in the area where a helicopter can land—and played football until we were all so bruised up and lame we could hardly come home. That's one of the reasons the Bhojpur boys stayed here until today. After Thanksgiving we had quite a time feeding all these people but managed all right since they were all used to eating rice. We had a wonderful time and got in a lot of bridge playing.

This morning while the boys were still here I got them all together to help me clip the teeth on my boar. Now the boar is about a year old and he's not too small; he can jump a three-and-half foot fence. We went after him, but he jumped out of the pen and led us a merry chase. Finally he ran in the front door and out the back door of our house into our ten-foot-wide back yard, all fenced in. The only place he could go from there was into Mac's room, which has an outside door. We finally caught him in there and brought him out with a leather strap in his mouth and tied him to a post. We had a huge audience watching us and we all took pictures. We found that none of our tools had enough leverage or were sharp enough to cut the teeth, so we sat on the pig until some clippers were sharpened. We had a great time. . . .

I'll be going into Kathmandu for Christmas, then take almost two months vacation, from the middle of January to the middle of February. I'm planning to trek out from Kathmandu to here with Peter Prindle who lives in Bhojpur. We plan to take the northern route and even get up to Namche Bazaar, which is the stepping off place for the Everest expeditions. Might pick up all sorts of Tibetan things up there.

December 14, 1963
Dhankuta

I've been to Terhathum and back since I last wrote to you. After
Thanksgiving, exams started at the high school and ours were
to be after a week, so we decided to leave for a week and go to
Terhathum, which is two days walk north of here. On Thursday
we started out. We had a ready-made porter, a man who had been
going out to the villages to get us eggs, who one week gambled
away all our egg money. He paid it back by carrying our stuff for
six days. We had a really nice trip, with full views of the mountains going both ways. Actually Terhathum is about the easiest
way to go from here; there's what is called a motorable road—
well—almost—but they can't get any jeeps to it. Anyway, it's a
good road for horses. In Terhathum we met the headmaster of the
high school, who is a really progressive man and the other teachers. They gave us a place to sleep and showed us around the town
and really treated us like royalty. We had brought along quite a
few teaching materials so the second afternoon we put on a little
demonstration. We made a mobile with solid geometry figures
we had whipped up out of some cardboard, then we got a piece
of flannel and put it against one wall and wrote English words on
pieces of paper and glued a piece of flannel on the back. These
stick to the flannel on the wall and are really great for teaching
English. That evening they brought us supper in our room—
chicken, rice, eggs, greens and pickle. Really good. In the evening
we sat around singing Christmas carols for them and listening to
their songs. The only bad thing about the trip was that my camera

was stolen, but we've got the police and the witch doctors working together on finding it so I'm fairly confident I won't see the damned thing again. I was getting tired of taking pictures anyway. On the way back we stopped at a middle school and stayed two hours and put up a flannel board and Barb made a phonetic chart for teaching the alphabet. There we saw the little boys grinding up old bricks and spreading the dust on boards. They practiced their writing on these with a little stick. It was much neater than using chalk and slate--and cheaper. On the trail we met a lot of men carrying guns. They had been down to Dhankuta to register them. We saw several muzzle-loading flint-locks—probably carried to Dhankuta every year for the last hundred years to be registered, and God knows how many times before that.

We met villagers along the way asking about our President being killed. I haven't told you before this the impact of the President's death on Nepal. It was really terrific and it shows the great respect of the people here for America. Ralph brought the news over Saturday morning after his death during our night here. We had planned a picnic with our Indian friends that day and they called it off, sending us their condolences. The school, which normally has a half holiday on Saturday declared a full holiday, and again gave a holiday on Monday, the day of mourning. We kept fairly close to our radio trying to find out what was happening. When we went out we were constantly asked about it, not only by teachers, but by some of our neighbors who can't read and write. Mac stopped in at a tea shop and heard the proprietor discussing it with one of his customers. The shopkeeper was telling the other fellow that he was foolish to think that there would be a lot of

Mike, Santa (Mac Odell), and Barbara Wylie. (Photographer unknown)

violence as an aftermath like in Vietnam. He said that everything would be peaceful. Mac said he was pretty pleased to know that the tea shop keeper understood how things were. Many people have wondered if it was a Negro or racist of some kind [who did it.] I was really overwhelmed by the interest and the feelings that I found in the people here.

We are planning a Christmas party here next Wednesday before we leave for Kathmandu; . . . We will probably have some problem with people not eating anything at our party. Boody, our cook, is a member of the butcher caste. This is about the lowest caste around here and most of the people in town won't take food from him. However we can't hire a Brahmin cook just to satisfy everyone in town and moreover, by doing so we would be encouraging the caste system which is not liked by the handful of progressive people here. There are some people who would like the opportunity to show the others that they don't care for caste. Anyway we are inviting all the teachers and important people in town. Some will come and some won't. Some will eat and some won't, but nobody will get angry over it or excited.

We will be flying into Kathmandu next Friday or Saturday and staying until after New Year's, then back here for the Bhojpur fair, then perhaps to western Nepal and then a trek back here from Kathmandu that should take me until the middle of February when I promise to write again.

Love, Mike

January 10, 1964
Friday
Okhaldhunga

Dear Folks,
Well, I'm off on a big trek, almost. We left Bhojpur on Sunday, after visiting the big fair/market there. I bought a few things there and I hope M.E. and Mom will like them. We had a fairly uneventful trip, reaching Okhaldungha about Wednesday noon. There are no Peace Corps here but there is a United Mission Dispensary where we're staying. Now we are getting ready to head north as soon as we can get two Sherpa porters. We had one Rai porter coming over here. But he didn't know the Sherpa language and didn't have enough clothes to go into the high country. We

may be going up to 15,000 feet (in January) so it will be cold. We will probably find porters tomorrow because it will be market day here and all sorts of people will be coming.

At the mission here there are a Scottish doctor, his wife and three children, two nurses (one is on leave now) and a Mennonite conscientious objector who is in charge of building a new dispensary, a building for patients, and three staff houses. He, Stan, is a pretty good fellow and doesn't go along with the song and dance of the others. He doesn't go to all their prayer meetings and everything. Pete and I are staying with him, sort of, and eating with the others. The doctor's family and Stan eat together and the nurses eat with a Nepali Christian couple who also work here. Last night we ate with Anne, the nurse, the Nepali couple, the head man of the village, and a Tibetan re-incarnated fellow who was passing through. We made quite a party. Although the Tibetan has been in Nepal for four years, he didn't speak as much Nepali as Pete and I, so we got along pretty well. He lives at a refugee camp a couple days north of here so we will be stopping in to see him on our way. We asked him about his family and if he would ever return to his home in Tibet. He just sort of made jokes about it but we could tell he really felt deeply about it. He talked about the Chinese for quite a while. We had a very interesting evening with these people.

On the way over here we met a Japanese mountain climber who is also going to Namche Bazaar. He has three Sherpa porters with him and will meet with his friends who are going there another way. He went with one of his porters a different way from us, so we sort of came along with the other two. The last night we stopped under some trees along the stream we were following and told our porter to cook rice while we went bathing. He was afraid to spend the night there but we convinced him it was safe and we thought it would be warm there (2,000 feet) before we climbed any higher. Pretty soon three *Chhretri* (warrior caste) brothers came along and they decided to stay there since we were there, otherwise they would be afraid. They were followed by a Newar-looking fellow who didn't say much and left suddenly. He was the topic of some conversation for the *Chhetris*. Next came a Sherpa who was about half dressed and didn't have anything with him, so he was busy making friends so that someone would give him something to eat and share their blanket with him. Next came the two Sherpas of the Japanese who had all Japanese equipment. This all must have made quite a picture. We ate first, with our hands, as we always do on the trail. Then the two Sherpas moved in with all their equipment and prepared an elaborate meal and ate with silverware. (Sherpas from the north use either silverware or chop-sticks, while most Nepalis use only their hands for eating.) Then the *Chhretris* pulled out some popped corn they had and lunched on that. They were all eyes at all the goings on; two of them were cross-eyed anyway. Then around the fire, Pete and I were speak-ing English, our porter was speaking in Nepali to the *Chhetris*, although his native language was Rai, the two Sherpa porters were speaking to each other in Sherpa language and the other little Sherpa was busy stoking the fire and bumming cigarettes. Once in a while we would all speak together in Nepali, which was the second language of everyone but the *Chhetris*.

We bought about 40 pounds of rice here and that should be

about enough for five days for us and two porters. We've been told that food is scarce north of here so we thought we should take some with us in case we can't find any. We also have the soups that you sent which are really handy. I really don't think you could have packed a better package to send here. Almost everything is going along with us. I'll probably write again from Kathmandu in about three weeks.

Love, Mike

April 7, 1964
Kathmandu

Today, being my last day in Kathmandu for another couple of weeks anyway, was a busy one. First thing, I took a hot shower, then I went to the Peace Corps office and signed the letter that the secretary there had typed for me to send to the Director of the Department of Agriculture. Then I went to the American Embassy to try to pick up my passport with its new Indian visa, but it wasn't ready so I went to the post office and bought their last two aerograms, then through the main bazaar a couple of times and out to see the Ambassador's wife, but she wasn't home, so I went to see the director of U.S. I.S. (Information Service, ie. propaganda, etc.) who had promised me some English teaching books when he came to Dhankuta with the Ambassador. I talked to him for half an hour, but he didn't have the books there so he told me to go to another building in the afternoon. Then I went to lunch at Jim Edwards' house. He is a British fellow who

works for U.S.A.I.D, who used to be in love with Barbara. After
that I went and picked up the books, and then went out to see
the Ambassador's wife again. She was about to go to a party but
we sat and talked for a little while. She's especially interested in
some book programs for adult literacy classes which the American
Women's Organization is sponsoring and she wanted to talk to
me a little about how the Peace Corps Volunteers might help in
the distribution of the books. We got that taken care of and then
I went over to see the wife of our Peace Corps Representative who
had a bunch of aerograms that she got stuck with and wanted to
sell. I managed to talk to her for half an hour, then went back to
the Peace Corps hostel with my load of books and then to the
office where they gave me about twenty pounds of mail to take
with me back to Eastern Nepal. Then I went to the dairy to get
some cheese, then back to the Embassy where they still didn't
have my passport ready, and then I went to the Goetze's for tea.
After tea, and a good chat with Ralph and Julie, it was already six
o'clock so I went to the Tibetan restaurant for some momos and
thongba, which was greasy as usual. That place isn't too clean. I
saw a rat running around there tonight, but no one got excited
about it. But it's cheap. And that was today, just like every day for
the last week. No wonder I like to get back to Dhankuta.

Now, to get back to your question about why I'm writing the
Director of the Department of Agriculture, and why I came in
to Kathmandu. Here's the story. A couple of weeks ago I wrote
a letter to our representative, telling him that I was considering returning to Nepal next fall for two more years in the Peace
Corps if I could change to the department of Agriculture and

do youth and extension work in a village. I got a radio-gram from him a few days later telling me to come to Kathmandu and talk it over. In my letter I told how I would like to obtain a little land (one to two acres) and a house in a village and to farm this trying some new seeds and methods, possibly maintaining a good cow, working with a few 4-H clubs in the surrounding villages, and working with some individual farmers on their own problems and perhaps keeping records on their enterprises. The representative was very excited about this idea, especially since the Peace Corps has been thinking along the same lines and hopes to bring in a whole group of youth workers about a year from now, and I would be sort of an experiment. The Director of the Department of Agriculture wasn't in town so I couldn't see him, so I wrote him a letter. He has to request me to come. Now I'm going back and tour the villages around Dhankuta to find a place which would fit my rather rigid requirements, and talk some rich land owner into giving me a little land. I hope to find my place within two weeks, so I can take my last two weeks vacation before all the business of termination.

I hope all this doesn't upset you too much. If it works out, I will be coming home pretty fast instead of the two or three months I once hoped to take. Anyway, the draft board doesn't give me much time, so either way I'll be coming home quickly and either way I will have a two-year job. I've been thinking of doing something like this for some time now, but I didn't really think seriously about it until about a month ago. I've been wanting for quite some time now, to get away from the schools and really get into some farming. I see so many possibilities for agriculture in

Terraced hillsides. (Mary Ellen Frame)

this country and no one is going to try out my ideas if I don't. So I'll be coming home this summer to pitch a little shit, and to gather a few seeds and a little more knowledge, and to make a little hay and have a wonderful summer at home.

We had a good time in Dhankuta when the Ambassador and his wife came to see us (she walked; he came by helicopter.) We had our servant cow-dung all the floors, and I baked brown bread and a couple of sour cream pies for the occasion—which is about as royal a welcome as we give anyone. They left us a big box of food that isn't locally obtainable, including a ham, cookies, cigarettes (none of us smoke) and a bottle of Scotch for Mac. We combined our ham with the Hambrick's so we had a nice big ham dinner for Easter, which also included raisin sauce for the

Terraced hillsides. (Mike Frame)

ham, potato salad, fruit salad, greens and cake. This was after the Ambassador left.

Since coming to Kathmandu, I've lived a gay life for a week and now it's time to go back to the hills.

Love, Mike

April 22, 1964
Dhankuta

When I got back to Dhankuta I went to see the local ag. extension worker and he had heard my plans from other sources. He had already talked to a rich fellow from one of the most

progress-minded villages and the man was willing to give me a
house, land and other help. The village is a good solid ten hours
walk from here, so the ag. worker would like me to go there
because he doesn't get time to go there very often himself as he
would like to. The next day I went out to see the village and
stayed with the school teachers there one day and returned the
third day. The man who would be giving me land was not there,
but I found a lot of very interested people. I thought it was a
pretty good place. Lots of good water, forest up above. All I need
now is approval from the Ag. Department.

Then I came back here for a couple of days before going off
to Chainpur on Peace Corps business. We are going to put two
teachers there in June. Chainpur is two easy days north of here
by either of the two normal routes, and it is two hard days from
here by either of the two routes I took. On my second day out I
took the road to Taplejung by mistake and climbed way up on a
ridge to about 10,000 feet. But I was not feeling bad because it
was so beautiful. The Rhododendron trees (some of them fifty
feet tall) were just past full bloom and still covered with blooms
ranging from almost white to the deepest red. The ground was
covered with blue violets and white wild strawberry blossoms and
then the view was terrific; the clouds would rise from the valleys
around and momentarily shut out the view and then they would
disappear and reveal the hills and valleys all around and the white
Himalayas in the distance. I didn't quite make it to Chainpur that
night but I stopped at a shelter about an hour down the hill. On
this trip I wore short pants and a tee shirt and took along a white
shirt and long pants for formal occasions. Also carried a change of

Arun River Valley. (Mary Ellen Frame)

underwear, socks, towel, sleeping bag, pen and paper, medicine, tooth brush, a loaf of brown bread, a bottle of peanut butter and a half dozen boiled eggs in my pack. This way I have a light pack and can buy bananas, milk and tea in the daytime to eat, and a supper in the evening. Well, the second night, stopping at the porter's shelter, I couldn't buy my supper all prepared; as a matter of fact I was all alone there. I reached Chainpur about 7:00 a.m. and talked to the head master about an hour and then left. Oh, by the way, I didn't go all the way to Taplejung; I met the road from Terhathum to Chainpur and took that.

On the return trip, after taking the wrong road out of Chainpur, I found myself somewhere north of there on the banks of the Arun River. There I asked a man how to get to Dhankuta and he said he didn't know except for going back to Chainpur. He reckoned it was about twenty-five *cos* (1 *cos* = 2 or 3 miles) which meant I had to walk fifty to seventy five miles to reach Dhankuta and it was already noon. Well, walking along the river, after three hours I met one of the usual roads and after another couple of hours I reached the town I was supposed to reach that night. At the shop there I met people from a village that Lee and I had visited a while back. They persuaded me to spend the night there and we had a great time. I also met a fellow who had been off to look at the girl that was proposed to be his wife. He said she was all right but that she didn't have an education. We decided to walk back together the next day. We got along well and he answered all the questions about me of the people along the trail so that I didn't have to. He invited me to his village, so although it was two or three more hours walking, I went with him and it was really nice. He brought out a royal feast for me and then took me around to see his fields and planting, and then to the local middle school. When we came back he asked me if I had a *khukuri* (knife—the national symbol.) I said no, so he brought one out and polished it up a little and gave it to me. He said it wasn't so good but that I had to take one to America with me.

Love, Mike

May 9, 1964
Kathmandu

I've been here in Kathmandu for almost two weeks now, but
it doesn't seem like it except that my money seems to be going
awfully fast. I've written my termination report and played a lot of
bridge. When I first came I had some round worms, but I think
they are pretty well gone now and I don't feel sickly anymore.
I've been staying at the Peace Corps hostel; now it's almost full
because most of our group is here for termination and the rest of
them will be in today. The place is really crowded with everyone
packing and every available place is filled with trunks and boxes.
Next week will be filled with things to do. There will be an audience with the King, then a two-day conference, language test and
another test, medical and dental examinations, besides packing
and travel arrangements, passports and visas—just to come home
for three or four months. . . . It is really hard to believe that my
term here is almost over with and that it's time to think about
coming home. Coming back to the over-developed world of auto-
mation and communication, where time is counted in seconds
and not in days is rather frightening to think about. Sometimes
we sit around and laugh about how out-of-place we are going to
feel when we get home. . . .

Now almost everyone is in Kathmandu for termination. It's
good to see them all again. I had hardly seen some of them for
almost two years except for a short time at Christmas time.

Hope you are all well and happy—don't wait for me to plant
the corn.

Love, Mike

Khatare, 1964–66

LETTERS

October 5, 1964
Dhankuta

Dear Bill and Sandy,

Since I'm interested in what's going on at home, I suppose you are interested in how my business is coming along. I wrote Mom and Dad last Thursday that I was about to leave here and go to Khatare and find out the score there. I left Dhankuta on Friday morning and reached Khatare late in the afternoon (walking for an hour in the rain with an umbrella.) John Franklin was with me. He had lived in that village for two weeks when he first arrived in Nepal and he couldn't believe that I would be able to live there for two years. We waited around for some time before Dumbir Bahadur came; he is the man rich enough to give me some land and rich enough to be the actual (if not in name) ruler of Khatare. Everyone paid some attention to what he said. He had a school teacher read aloud the letter which we brought from Madan, the Ag. J.T.A. (Junior Technical Assistant) in Dhankuta, telling about me and what I wanted. Soon we were walking around the village looking at different pieces of land. He suggested one piece of land and said I could live in a couple spare rooms in a house by the school. I spotted a small house on the other side of the field he had pointed out and asked if anyone was living there. He said it was empty. We immediately went over to look at it. It was one of a very few vacant houses I have seen in Nepal. It is a good little house with thick, well-plastered, stone and mud walls and a thatched roof. The two stories measure about ten by fifteen feet inside and the ceilings are high enough to stand comfortably. The rooms were a little bit dark, with only one small window (with shutters) on each floor, but I can make another one or two on the second floor. There is also a small porch in front, and a thatched roofed shelter behind. I think I can make it into a pretty comfortable pad. The land lies on sloping terraces, sloping toward the north. I was a little bit leery of that but the next day I found that the sun hit this land most of the day although there are some trees up the hill a little way. I told them that I only wanted a small portion of the land this winter, but would want more next spring for planting corn. There are also two or three small patches of land behind the house more under the trees that I don't know what to do with. I'll get my water from an improved spring just down the hill and for a bath I can go to a beautiful stream about a thousand feet down.

Now all I need are a few tools and a good servant. I won't be going out there until after the holidays which start soon and last two weeks; I guess I'll just be diddling around for awhile. After I get everything ready, maybe I will take a trip somewhere.

One thing I was going to do while I was home was to get a bunch of pictures of animals and things. Maybe you could do this for me Sandy. Cut some big pictures (pretty) of cows and pigs and other animals and vegetables, fruits and crops from magazines. Include things which the people here might be familiar with. Then when you send them to me I can put them up on my walls. I also need a ball of string sometime.

We had a bad trip back from Khatare. We were at the bottom of the worst hill about eleven in the morning and boy was the sun hot. We had to climb for more than three hours—straight up about five thousand feet. When we got up on the ridge we were soaked with sweat and got hit by a blast of cold air and clouds. We really got chilled. That's life. I hope you are all getting along all right.

Love, Mike

October 16, 1964
Dhankuta

Dear Mom and Dad,

I expect that you read my letter to Bill and Sandy telling them about my visit to Khatare, and how I would have to wait until after the two-week holidays before I could move in out there. I'm still sort of sitting it out. Last Friday two new volunteers for Chainpur arrived along with the P.C. doctor, so I decided to go along to Chainpur with them. Well, it was quite a trip. It took us two and a half days getting there and everyone but me was done in by the trip. We stayed the afternoon and night there, getting the boys settled. They will be teaching in the school. I also bought some brass plates there. On the way back, the doctor and I took a shorter trail which, although quite a bit easier, some people thought was more dangerous. Going to Chainpur we had followed the ridge top—getting up to probably nine thousand feet. But going back, most of the way we followed the Arun river. The doctor developed a bad knee when we first started downhill, so it wasn't much fun for him. When we first reached the Arun, we had a big stream to cross. It was still swollen from the rains (which I think are finally over) and was pretty swift. We took off our pants and hoisted up our packs and tackled it together, holding each other's arm. We stepped in and found the bottom was large rocks which were not secure in the current. We were waist deep, four legs braced together against the current and inching our way across one step at a time. It was a good ten yards to the other side and it seemed to take an age. When we pulled out on the other side I was shaking from the tension. Then we crossed miles of sandy banks and across rice fields and up above the river clinging to footholds in the cliffs, where the river came to the walls of the gorge. It was a fairly uneventful two-day trip otherwise.

Mac and Barbara came to Dhankuta last night and will be staying here three or four days until they can get porters to go up north with them. It is good to see them again.

I will be going out to Khatare probably on October 21. I want to be there in time for the Jitpur market (four hours away) which happens on the days of full moon and new moon. I'm going to have to do some remodeling work on the house and plant some vegetables right away, besides breaking in a new servant, so I will have plenty to do for awhile. The house is small, so I won't have

too much trouble furnishing it. I'm really getting anxious to get out there and get to work. People keep asking me what I am going to accomplish and I'm not sure myself. I still have a lot of ideas kicking around in my head but I don't know how they will work out. I've decided to have a combined latrine-compost pit, which may or may not be acceptable to the people, because it will probably be my only source of manure. I've also been toying with the idea of placing the compost under the corn rows when I plant, rather than broadcasting it. It would be quite a bit more work, but it might pay off with bigger yields.

I am getting tired of just sitting around thinking about these things and not doing anything. Probably some of my ideas are a bit unrealistic also from being away from the farming.

Well, I certainly hope I get some news from the other side of the world one of these days. I got a good "Grundig" radio in Hong Kong and I'm getting all the world news, but they don't tell much about the home front.

Love, Mike

November 28, 1964
Khatare

Merry Christmas!

I'm sending you something to print in your Christmas letter. Thanksgiving was pretty good. . . . I got hold of a large honeycomb-type oven which was used previously by a restaurant man who baked bread. I made about a dozen loaves of brown bread

Trail along the Arun River. (Mary Ellen Frame)

and four pies and put them all in at once. We had three roast chickens for dinner with chestnut dressing. There were only ten of us. I got back here just at dark last night. Hope you find this printable:

I want to wish all of my friends on the other side of the world a Merry Christmas. Santa will not find so many stockings hung for him here, but nevertheless he will fill what he finds about twelve hours before he will get to those in Minnesota.

I'm planning to spend Christmas with the two people I lived with last year. They have moved to the north country, so I will have to walk five or six days to get there. I think the trip will be worth it because they live in one of the most beautiful parts of Nepal, with pine forests, pastures and the snowy peaks not so far away.

Some of you may be wondering what I am doing here. If so, you aren't alone—sometimes I wonder about it myself. Actually I am an experiment to see if the Peace Corps can do anything for the agriculture of Nepal. A former program had Peace Corps Volunteers in higher positions in the Department of Agriculture. That program was somewhat unsuccessful, so they are trying my project, where I am at the bottom of the Department of Agriculture, almost as an ordinary farmer. So I have come to live for two years in a farming community. I have a small house and an acre or two of land where I can try out new methods, new varieties of seeds and even entirely new crops. I also visit the farmers around the community and advise them, but I think my own demonstration will be more effective. It is easier to show farmers than to teach them. They tend to believe more. Also, I don't know for sure what methods are best here or what varieties of seed will work until I try them.

I feel that agriculture is very important here, since Nepal is in a position where she can help to feed the starving masses of India. But I am not here because of any great dedication, but because I have become very interested in the possibilities in agriculture here where machines and commercial fertilizer are out of the question and where the land which has no topsoil gives back little more than is put into it. Moreover, I enjoy my life here, especially the people with their strange ways, never hurried and not wanting some of the comforts which we think are so necessary. I wish I could send each of you a poinsettia from here, but they are too big. The people here use them for fences along the trails and they grow about twenty feet tall. The huge blossoms are really beautiful

at this time of year. Anyway, I'll wish you a Merry Christmas collectively, although I can't individually.

Yours, Mike

January 31, 1965

Khatare

. . . I went into Dhankuta the other day just to get my mail and
see the fellows and I ended up running around all day long, doing
things that had to be done. In the process, I got my money from
the bank; it takes at least an hour to cash a check. I got my ration
of sugar and also picked up forty fruit trees and found a porter to
bring them out. These were apple, walnut, peach and pear—all
good varieties from Kathmandu, which I thought the people in
the higher parts of this area were crying to get. Friday I came back
and since I was carrying twenty-five to thirty pounds myself, it
took me eight hours. Yesterday, I took half the trees and went up
(an hour's fast climb) directly behind Khatare to Tayloong and
Kapring. I expected to have some trouble keeping all the trees
from being taken by the first person I met, but it was just the
opposite. Nobody seemed to want to take any of the trees. I'm
sure they would have been more than happy to take them if I had
given them free, but I had to charge what I had paid for them.
They'll take better care of them also if they've paid for them. I
ended up trading four trees with one fellow for about 2 pecks of
millet and with another fellow for two dozen eggs. In all, I got
rid of ten trees. Today I should have gone up to Goomaune and

Mulkarka above Marek to distribute the rest of the trees, but I
woke up lazy, so I walked over to Marek and had a note sent up
telling that I had the trees; if anyone wanted them they could
come and get them. If I don't get rid of them in the next couple
of days I will plant them here and get rid of them next winter. My
next deal of this sort is to get together an order for orange and
tangerine trees from the farmers of the lower areas so that the fruit
farm will reserve some for us. This will also be a task—I never was
much good as a salesman. . . .

February 14, 1965
Khatare

. . . Every day someone brings me some new problem to solve
for them. Typical of this was an old man who came to me the
day before yesterday talking about something that was eating all
his bananas and also would eat corn. We talked for half an hour
or so and I found out that it wasn't insects or some kind of bird.
I finally went to his home with him and he took me out and
showed me the monkeys. I hadn't seen any monkeys around here
before and he was using a different name for them than is usual;
the thought of monkeys just never entered my mind. Then we had
to discuss the ethical question of killing them. Monkeys in Kathmandu aren't killed because of their godliness. There is a monkey
god, Hanuman, who led the monkeys and saved somebody's life
or kingdom or something, and so they are sort of considered
sacred. Well, this old man wasn't going to settle for that, since

they had been stealing his corn and bananas for years. He wanted them killed! It became rather obvious that the monkeys in Kathmandu are a different kind than these. We both agreed to this; then we had to discuss the technical aspects of killing them. Guns and bows are out because the monkeys immediately scatter when they see these and even if one or two are killed, the rest of the herd will come back to eat the bananas. Monkeys are too smart for traps and normal ways of giving poison. Fencing to keep them out would be almost impossible. The only thing I could think of is a liquid poison, which could be injected into the bananas, but this is dangerous because boys also steal bananas. This took my afternoon and nothing was solved, but I know where to get help and maybe we can solve it—if the Agriculture Department also agrees that this kind of monkey can be killed. . . .

I've been learning more skills lately. Thatching my house last week was my first experience at such a task. We bought $2.00 worth of grass (fifteen huge loads,) ten bamboo and hired three men for two days to help us. The bamboo was cut in one-inch strips and used to hold down each row of grass. We also had to cut bamboo ties to tie things down. Then we had to sort through the old thatch for usable portions, tie these in bundles (straw ties) and cut them off even, to be used for the border (just as we put a double row of shingles at the edge [of the roof at home.]) I took the occasion to introduce the pitchfork, which arrived in my surface freight last week, piercing my Bible. I hastily made a six-foot handle for it and used it to toss up the bundles of grass. The bundles were small, so I could easily toss three or four at a time, much more quickly than tossing them by hand, much to the annoyance of the man on the roof, who was trying to catch them before they rolled off. I also took the occasion to put a new top section on my chimney—a tin pipe with a small roof over it. . . .

March 30, !965
Khatare

I'm just sitting here by the kitchen fire waiting for the rice to cook, so I guess it's a good time to write to you. It has been another day where accomplishment has been small or at least it seems small. Sometimes I wonder how I get any work done at all around here with all the people coming. All together, I had twelve separate visitors today who stayed more than five minutes each. I'll give you a run-down. Just before 6:00 AM, I was awakened by a neighbor who had some bananas to sell and also wanted some iodine to treat his daughter's goiter (no iodine.) After that I started digging in the garden and abruptly a teacher came. I came in to have tea with him and found him reading a book out loud. Before we had our tea, another man came to get some rat poison (which I am selling.) He stayed for tea and talked with me about insects in his tangerine trees and about getting an apple tree, which I'll be getting for him next winter. We also talked about the pile of charred bones, which were on my porch and how he could use them in his orchard. After breakfast I started crushing the bones with a block of wood and a young blacksmith came, also wanting rat poison but he had no money so he borrowed my *khukuri* knife instead. Then came the man with a case of boils on his buttock, which I have treated a couple of times before. I got

Thatching a house. (Mike Frame)

Thatching a house. (Mike Frame)

tired of pounding the bones with the wood block and so Bhim, my new servant, and I took what was left of the bones to the landlord's house and pounded them in their rice mill. The women were a bit squeamish about us using their mill for bones and insisted that we besmear the place with cow dung when we were finished. We ended up with forty pounds of bone meal as fine as flour. After that I went back to the garden where I was digging a place to plant tomatoes. (Removing the quack grass made it a job.) Then came a woman who wanted some peas for her dying father, my milkman who needed some nails (which I provided,) also a hammer to hit the nails with and several school boys each coming separately and watching me for half an hour or so. I finally did manage to get about two dozen tomatoes transplanted, well fertilized with ashes and bone meal, and in the process, I taught three or four people your method, Mom, of planting them. That brought me around to almost supper time so I sat and shot the bull with a couple left-over neighbor boys and then went to the spring to wash up.

Chicken business isn't all profit in Nepal either. Of the twenty-nine chickens I bought two weeks ago, I now have four. There is a strange little animal here called a Malsanpro, which I gather is somewhat like a weasel, but twice as vicious. First it got in the chicken house and took five and left ten dead. Of the remaining eleven (two had been sold to a friend and one crushed by a door before that) one was sick and was quickly taken by a hawk not more than ten feet from me. Then there were ten. We put them for the night under my (Grandfather Frame's) trunk which is topless and upside down, used as a seat on my porch. Then I went off to Dhankuta. When I got back, the first thing I saw was a hole in the porch floor (which is made of hard-packed clay and rock) going under the trunk. Well, we now have the remaining four sleeping under a basket in the corner of the kitchen. I've also requested a good dog from the Peace Corps.

April 4, Dhankuta

My how time flies. But the last four days have been busy. I decided to go into Kathmandu (a trip I had planned on for a long time) right away, without waiting to harvest the wheat as I had planned. Bhim, my new servant, is working out better than any expectations and I have left him to finish up the plowing and corn planting and planting of some summer vegetables while I'm gone.

I've been wanting to get to Gorkha and see what a mission farmer is doing out there; I also feel that it is time for me to get away from the village for awhile; I haven't been to Kathmandu for six months. And right now I'm in a slightly rundown condition, and I can get a good physical in Kathmandu. I think I have worms. No diarrhea, but lots of gas!

I came about halfway to Dhankuta yesterday and spent the night in Siduwa, a collection of tea shops on the ridge top road. We had a hell of a storm in the late afternoon—hail, rain and cold winds, but I was safely inside for the whole show. In the morning when I started walking, the air was clear and there were whole new mountains covered with snow that I hadn't seen, or at least not noticed before. It was a beautiful walk. . . .

Love, Mike

Bhim Bahadur Rai. (Mike Frame)

April 11, 1965
Khatmandu

Returning to Kathmandu after six months in the hills wasn't quite
like returning to America from Nepal, but it has its similarities.
The Americans here are all scurrying around and are too busy
in the daytime to sit down and spend half an hour in conversation and the evenings are filled with dinners, parties and movies.
The traffic has increased tremendously in the city and there are
tourists all over the place. Two and a half years ago there wasn't
much traffic and tourists were so uncommon that we would usually stop and talk to them. On the main street, (The King's Way)
there are now a German and an Indonesian Embassy which didn't
exist before. I've spent the last few days waiting to get a seat on a
plane to Ghorka and also recovering from my stomach trouble,
which made me feel like a blimp with two exhaust pipes, but no
diarrhea. I am almost fully recovered now, although I have one
day left of the five-day treatment. I had a thing called "Giardia,"
which is, I think, a one-celled protozoan.

I've had several invites out to dinner the last few days and I also
made a trip out to Bhaktapur and saw a lot of old friends. I'll have
to write to Budri about that. There are now two pretty nice P.C.
girls living in my old house there. They seem pleased and happy
with the situation in Bhaktapur, but being girls, I don't envy their
situation there. Bhaktapur is probably the most conservative area
in Nepal and the women are definitely in a lower position. They
have a difficult time finding any friends among the women folks
in town because there are very few educated and a good share of

them don't even speak Nepali. I think Bhaktapur is the only place I have seen in Nepal which hasn't changed appreciably in the past two years.

The new years festival (Bisket Jatra) was just about to get under way. . . .

I've just moved out to the airport where there is likely to be at least an hour's wait so I ought to be able to finish this. I'm going to visit the mission in Appipal. They have an agricultural station there which has been functioning for several years independently of the Agriculture Department. I expect to learn quite a bit in the two days that I stay there. The Ag. Department is pretty limited in what they can do for me. The missionaries are more in the practical line.

The airport is really busy today and overcrowded because two flights are being held up because of overcast airports in other places. A big planeload of tourists just came in from Delhi and another planeload is getting ready to fly on out—all American little old ladies on a round-the-world tour.

I'm hoping to sneak through the immigration check today since my passport is in the Embassy being renewed and getting new Nepali and Indian visas. I hope it won't be too hard. I used to be friends with the chief inspector here but he got transferred. If he was here I wouldn't worry. It really is silly to need a passport for purely internal flights. There is a new, longer runway being constructed here now. It will be nice when something more than DC3s can fly in and out. But jets still won't be able to land; the valley is too small, although they could make a runway long enough. Well, my plane came in so I guess I'll be flying soon. I have to find a place to mail this soon.

I hope you are getting into shape for coming over here.

I've just got authorization to purchase a horse; that should be better for getting around. I'm afraid I'd have to run my legs off without it. Another P.C. teacher will be living in the same village with me now. He is Larry Leamer.

Love, Mike

April 17, 1965
Kathmandu

Well, seven months of my second term in Nepal is finished and I am even more excited about my job than ever before. I went out to the United Mission in Appipal (near Gorkha) and arrived there in the evening after a half-hour flight and a three-hour walk. There I found three men working in agriculture. One is a middle-aged Canadian named Herman who reminded me somewhat of my uncle by the same name, with his back-woodsy way of talking and living, but having a good mind which isn't overrun with little problems. The other two are Germans, one of whom is a veterinarian and both bright young fellows, speaking German, English or Nepali fluently. They took time to show me all that they are doing and let me in on their mistakes and their hopes. They are experimenting with corn, wheat and other grains, grafting fruit trees, and running an agricultural supply store. They have built a silo and are in the process of building a barn. They have quite a few chickens, two buffalo and some rabbits and will soon be getting a shipment of milking goats from Israel. They don't have all the advantages. They have no irrigation and they have less land than I have. The thing that was most impressive was the way they had farmers who were accustomed to buying things from them, fish meal for chickens, bone meal for fertilizer (which they make) and different varieties of seeds and insecticides. They told me how to make a silo, how to make German sausages, and how to tell the difference between the small grains by looking at the leaves. I stayed there about three days, getting back to Kathmandu Thursday night. Yesterday I had a physical exam and the doctor said I was in top physical shape, although a little underweight from my recent sickness. I also got a Peace Corps jeep to haul me all over town and had some good discussions with some A.I.D. agriculturalists. I'm pretty well loaded down with seeds now and I have a better idea of the role I have to play.

HAPPY BIRTHDAY MOM

I met Dorothy Mierow yesterday—she had just come in for the Easter weekend. We had some common experiences to talk about. She said she felt just like Rip Van Winkle coming back here; there is such a fast turnover in Americans around here that we don't know many people any more.

I'll be leaving here on Tuesday and I will hope to get back to Khatare either Thursday or Friday. I'm going to stop in Dhankuta on Thursday and buy some meat and intestines in the market to make bologna with.

Easter Sunday

Yesterday turned out to be a very interesting day. We went out
to Godavari, which is on the southern rim of the valley. There is
a Catholic boys school there, which is easily the best school in
Nepal. What we were mainly interested in was Father Saboule's
beekeeping activities. He took us to his hives, opened them up
and showed us the frames, taking them out gently, and explaining everything to us as we went. It was really quite interesting
and he explained to me how I could keep them in a cavity in the
wall of my house. Then he showed us his flower gardens, orchids,
gas-producing cow dung tank and all the school buildings. Quite
impressive! We had lunch there and then came back for a Peace
Corps wedding which was held in a garden. Very nice. I knew the
groom, but the bride just came over to marry him and take a job
at a mission hospital in the town where he lives.

I went to the sunrise service this morning and it was very
nice. They served coffee and goodies after it so it was doubly
worthwhile.

Love, Mike

May 26, 1965
Dharan

Here I am in the British Army hospital in Dharan and nobody
knows what's wrong with me, or if there is anything wrong with
me. I came in a week ago with a pain in my lower abdomen,
which I was afraid was going to be a hernia, but they said I had

some infection and it was nothing to worry about. Because I was also having some intestinal problems, they decided to run the full course of tests on me and give me a good going over, but they haven't found anything wrong yet. I should be ready to go back in a few days. The weather is really hot here, but I'm in a private, air-conditioned room so it is all right. We are getting some pre-monsoon rains now every two or three days which cools things off for a little while. The low-altitude trails are pretty hard with all this heat; it has to be either early morning or late afternoon when we walk now. I expect summer is well upon you now also and I wouldn't really mind coming home to help with the haying for awhile—I sure enjoyed it last summer. . . .

I've read half a dozen books and now I'm busy writing a report on my job for the Agriculture Department and the Peace Corps. Writing an impressive report is difficult because my job is sort of ambiguous and progress, of course, is very slow. I feel strongly that the Ag. Dept. and the P.C. should be thinking about a project along these lines in the future. I think this is the best way that the P.C. can make a contribution to the agriculture of this country. Here in Asia, close to the hungry masses of India, agriculture is the part of the economy which needs the most improvement. Do you know how much wheat the U.S. is sending to India these days? 100,000 tons per *day*. Ocean freighters are being continually unloaded in Calcutta and this is just a drop in the bucket; people are still hungry! This will have to increase until the time when strong birth control measures begin to show their effect. This leaves Nepal with pockets of starvation, since it is easier for areas of surplus to export to India rather than to send the excess grain to other areas in Nepal. The trade routes run north and south, not east and west.

June 6, 1965
Khatare

. . . On Thursday, at the Dhankuta market, I got up real early and bought about ten pounds of meat (pork and buffalo) just as they were cutting it up. Along with the meat, I got about ten or fifteen feet of buffalo intestines. I cleaned the intestines and put the meat in brine for an hour or two, then I carried it out here (Khatare.) On Friday I ground it all up, mixed in a lot of spices and put it in the gut, which I had turned inside-out. Needless to say, this turned into quite a project, me not knowing how to handle these slimy guts, which would burst just as I was getting them firmly packed. Well, I ended up with three nice baloney-sized rings, plus about ten shorter links. Then these had to be smoked for about a day. If I was in America, I would have to charge about five dollars for one of these rings, but since my time isn't worth anything here, I can afford to eat them. And I did eat a small one. It was about the best sausage I've ever had—sort of like a mild pepperoni—I'll have to use it on pizza.

There was quite a bit of interest among the local people watching me make this. They had never seen or heard of it before. I didn't know myself if it were really possible for awhile. New discoveries every day.

Village boy. (Mike Frame)

June 12, 1965
Khatare

. . . It's a beautiful morning here today, with all the corn and trees so bright and green after the rain and the patches of cloud or fog moving up the hillsides out of the valleys. The sun has just come out now and the sky is so blue in places. The birds and insects are making their usual sounds; I can hear the pleasant sound of people's voices in the neighboring houses and a foot-treadle rice mill going "thud, thud, thud," up at my landlord's. A girl just came to sell me some bananas, which makes the morning completely wonderful. She had a big bunch, twenty-three all together, so after eating one to find out how it tasted, I bought them for about a penny each. The bananas here come in about a hundred varieties and even within a named variety the taste can range from bitter to disagreeable to very sweet and delicious. Some are small, others long; some thin, others fat as a fist. These today were no bigger around than my ring finger and about eight inches long. The long kind are sometimes bitter, but these were as good as the two-inch long, sweet variety. Sometimes the bananas are good except for a woody core or perhaps some seeds in the middle, which makes eating them difficult.

It is evening now after a rain in the afternoon and it's equally as beautiful as it was this morning. I went down to watch my neighbors planting their rice nursery beds. It is quite a chore, having to plow two or three times and then harrow a couple of times, plus re-building the dikes and bringing in water by irrigation ditch. As they work, the fields fill up with water and just before they sow the rice, they go through smoothing it all with their hands under six inches of water, and removing the weeds. I told them they should have borrowed my rake for that, but they were already through, although they thought it was a good idea. They were in a big hurry to get done today, since tomorrow is full moon day and they can't plow with the bulls then.

A nice sort of fellow stopped in here today and I guess my house has now become a hospital. He came with stomach trouble (the same as everyone else around here) and wanted some medicine. Since he doesn't live anywhere around here, I put him to bed for awhile this afternoon and he woke up too late to leave, so he is here for supper and for the night. I don't mind this sort of thing anymore; I just wish I had a little more medicine and a little

Hill village. (Mary Ellen Frame)

more knowledge of what to do. A woman came to me yesterday
with a cut going in between her thumb and finger almost an inch
deep and about as long. I decided it needed a couple of stitches,
so I took my needle and thread, took one stitch and it hurt her
so badly she wouldn't let me take another. It looked much better today when she came back for a clean bandage. I really got
nervous while I was trying to work on it. It was made by a cow's
horn. . . .

June 20, 1965
Dhankuta

. . . I was quite surprised and happy to receive three copies of
"Organic Gardening and Farming" magazine and two pamphlets
on organic fertilizers from the same people. I expect that you
wrote to them, Dad. Are they going to continue to send these—is
there a subscription or is this all? It is really an interesting magazine for where I am at. I have to snicker every once in a while at
their anti-chemical beliefs—the way they sneer at most of the
scientific work being done at agriculture colleges and experiment
farms across the nation, but for where I am in Nepal, I can get
a lot of information from these crackpots. I think their methods
of treating insects without insecticides are especially interesting
and may be helpful since insects are my greatest problem. Who
knows, maybe garlic planted between the cabbages will keep off
the worms! It would sure make life easier. . . .

I expect you are having a great summer as usual, plenty of hard
work, long days, good food and sunshine. I sure enjoyed it there
last summer. But I think Americans work far too hard to main-
tain all their machinery and luxuries. It's funny that these farmers
in Nepal have no machinery and few conveniences but they can
get a living off their little plots by working hard only in certain
seasons and laying around the rest of the time. Only the women
here work fairly steadily, but even most of their work is only time
consuming and not very hard. And if you make the comparison
about the white-collar worker, or businessman, you'll find that the
upper class American works just as hard, although he is wealthy,

whereas the Nepali who is a notch above the rest will do nothing, if possible.

July 5, 1965
Khatare

. . . Since the monsoon is well established, there's really not very much to do. But the less I have to do, the busier I seem to be. The medical business has been strong lately with my neighbor who fell off his roof and a four-month-old baby who rolled into the fire and badly burned both his feet. I've been freshly bandaging both these people every day for over a week now and so they are doing all right. The baby had a temporary set back because one of his uncles came and decided that modern medicine wasn't the thing. He removed the bandages, killed a chicken and put the warm blood on the burns. I guess it probably didn't hurt very much except that the bandages always stick where the dried blood wasn't removed. . . .

Most people are busy picking corn and planting rice in the same fields just as fast as possible. It is quite an operation; before the corn is ready, they go in and cut down the sides of the terraces, making the walls nice and smooth and leaving the weeds all in the middle; they also mend the rims of the terraces and ditches. Then at the appointed time they start picking corn at the top of a man's land. At this time, slightly over half of the corn is ripe enough to be dried; the rest will be eaten roasted. The corn is picked; the top halves of the stalks are carried home for the cows; the bottom halves are thrown out of the way; the water is pouring in. . . . The whole operation moves down the hill as the terraces fill with water and overflow into the lower terraces. . . .

I'm making a big compost heap with the horse manure and all the weeds that are available now. I have eight kinds of corn growing or planted, two kinds of soybeans, three kinds of cow peas, local and American peanuts, five kinds of green beans, mangels, sunflower, okra, peppers and beets all doing well. The tomatoes, squash, melons, pumpkins and cucumbers have all been attacked by mildew and eaten by insects. I also have two kinds of legumes for green manure and a patch of six-foot tall giant Napier grass, which everyone thinks is sugar cane. Among these things I have about 500 species of local weeds all growing nicely. The pole beans that did so well and I left for seed have done just that. Before the pods turned yellow and dried out for me to pick for seed, the seeds all germinated so that when I go to pick them, all I find is a pod full of bean sprouts. I guess I'll have to try again this fall. . . .

July 29, 1965
Khatare

We have had almost a week without rain since I came back from Dhankuta. (I went to Dhankuta July 6, waited for the Peace Corps doctor to arrive—he was late. On July 12 I took a new volunteer up to Terrathum, went back to Dhankuta and came home July 20.) I have been working like mad trying to get caught up on things while I had good weather. My servant, Bhim, went home to help plant rice and I'm not sure if he will come back or not. If not, I'll have to wait until rice planting is over before I can find someone else. It is pretty hard here without someone to at least cook and take care of the little chores. Yesterday it was New Moon day so I got up early (as usual with the first bit of light) and did my floors with cow dung; I follow local custom and do this according to the moon. The floors need it every two weeks anyway. Then I had some breakfast and went off to the Jitpur market. This could be called a holiday, if it wasn't two hours walk each way and a lot of haggling and arguing in between. But it was a good market yesterday and I had my bag full coming home. I bought about a peck of peaches (about the size of apricots,)a pineapple, an 18-inch long cucumber, a couple pounds of pork, three or four pounds of rice, a coconut, a clay pot, and a couple dozen eggs. There were some other things I would like to have bought, but I had no way of carrying any more, and no companion.

It started raining about six o'clock this morning, just after I got out in the field to do some work. It has rained about an inch now and I am enjoying some rainy-day jobs. Today I'm making hominy and it is sort of fun although I don't know what I'm doing, or what I'm going to do with this big pot of hominy when I get done—I don't think it will keep very long. Anyway it is nice keeping the fire burning low while I fool around with odd jobs. I don't think I'll make hominy too often; it is pretty hard on the fuel supply and it takes a lot of water also which I don't like to carry in the rain.

I've been picking corn lately and seeing how things are shaping up. I think I've learned quite a bit, this year, about growing corn here. The only non-local corn (of the several I planted) which looked at all decent, was popcorn, whose seed was purchased at the Red Owl store—a five-pound bag, which I was going to eat, but planted some. It could make a significant contribution since it bears as well or better than local corn and is about two weeks earlier (75–90 days.) The only problem is the loose husk which makes it easy prey for insects, birds, etc. Nepali corn has very tight husks which are desirable here where it is stored with the husk on, and tied together and hung by the outer husks. My sweet corn is almost entirely destroyed by corn borers and ear worms, partly because it was planted later.

Now is the season to get started on my winter vegetables: peas, carrots, cabbages, tomatoes. Soybeans look great, sweet potatoes are coming along and sunflowers are in full bloom. I'm going to try a few oats right now since I think they will grow in this damp cool weather and will ripen in the fall when it is sunny and dry.

The rain seems to be slowing down now; I guess I'd better get the horse out, get some water, and do some more odd jobs. It is funny; no one has come today; usually if I was trying hard to get some work done there would be hordes. I've been getting rid of a lot of rat poison lately; all sorts of people are finding that the rats are eating the corn just as fast as it is being harvested. A half a rupee isn't too much money to pay to be rid of them. Next week the rice planting will be about finished so my visitors will be increasing. In a couple of days, I will try to send a boy into Dhankuta to pick up some stuff for me, including my pay check, and he will take this letter. I don't feel like going in myself for a while now.

Love, Mike

November 3, 1965
Paphlu, Solu

Dear Dave and Claire,
Well, here I sit in Paphlu, Solu, huddled up in my sleeping bag
trying to keep warm enough to write to you. I'm on vacation!
Having a wonderful time; wish you were here! I decided to walk
into Kathmandu and to stop off here and get cooled off on the
way. From Dhankuta it took me five days to get here, although
I had hoped to make it in just four. But without a map, I didn't
figure this new route to be as long as it was and then I got lost a
few times and had some bad weather.

On my third day out I was travelling alone, after getting direc-
tions from a friendly shepard. I had to go along a trail above a cliff
of about 2,000 feet, then drop down to a stream, cross and go up
the other side. I was fine walking along in the pine forest above
the cliff, then the road began to go downhill and pretty soon there
was the inevitable fork in the road, with no one around for miles.
I took the most likely road, which turned out to lead to a patch of
rice fields and finally down to the river. But there was no crossing
there and no trail up the other side. So I started to walk downstream along the edge, not being able to wade this raging, ice cold
stream. Finally there was no space to walk along the river and I
found myself doing some pretty difficult climbing around the face
of the rock, hanging on with my finger tips and toes to holes in
the slippery rock. I finally got to an impasse and had to retrace
my steps for about half an hour and then plunge upward into the
woods. Up above it had been nice open pine forest, but along the

stream it was *jungle*—six feet high grass, briers, nettles and a few leeches to take care of my extra blood. I worked my way along on the narrow strip between the river gorge, and the 2,000 foot cliff that I wanted to stay beneath, cutting my way through the undergrowth with my *khukuri* knife as it began to rain and get dark. There I was, trying to find a place to sleep in the middle of the wet wilderness. I finally found a dry spot underneath an overhanging rock, cleared out the rubbish and small rocks, laid out my sleeping bag, ate my stale waffles, flattened rice and peanuts and went to bed. The next morning, after two or three hours of wandering through the undergrowth, I came upon a small patch of rice fields and an old man who was sitting there watching over them. He happily listened to my story and took me down the hill, across a simple log bridge, and up the other side. So there I was, all lost and found again and only about a day wasted.

Here I am staying in a big Sherpa house where Mac and Barbara (my old housemates in Dhankuta) live with a rich family. Actually the place is like a feudal manor house with its many large rooms, high ceilings and plank floors, huge kitchen with a great fire burning at all times, but since the room is about the size of the south end of our old barn, and full of drafts, it is always cold except by the fire. They have stables and high stone fences with huge gates, about fifteen feet high with a little roof over them. They have two or three regular house servants but when there is field work to do they have huge gangs of twenty or so people out in the fields with the mother watching over them. Actually there are only two people of the regular family here—the mother who runs the household and the son of twenty-five or so who takes care of the government of the area. The other sons have gone to live in separate households here or in Kathmandu.

Tomorrow we are going up to the *Gompa* (Bhuddist monastery) for the biggest celebration of the year. It goes on for 15 days, but it will climax now with three days of dancing by all the monks. We will just go up there (a couple of hours from here) and stay for the three days. This is the biggest Gompa in Nepal and its head lama is very holy, being a thirteenth reincarnation, having been a high lama in each incarnation. After this is over, I'll try to get to Kathmandu as fast as possible, probably four or five days, but it will be just after full moon, so I'll be able to get up in the wee hours of the morning and get a good start by moonlight. I'll probably carry this letter with me and mail it in Kathmandu when I get there, since I'll be moving as fast as the mail runners. Hope you are well, and still getting along with each other.

Love, Mike

December 5, 1965
Khatare

Well, here I am sitting in the little round house I made last year to keep pigs in, but never got any pigs. I read all the bulletins about sweet potatoes and it says when they are first put in storage, the store room should be heated to eighty degrees and the humidity should be ninety to ninety-five degrees for about a week. I'm trying to approximate that and here I am sitting by the fire with a big pot of water on it and three boxes full of nice big sweet potatoes beside me. I wonder if it will work. The sweet potatoes were a major accomplishment. It was the bone meal I used for fertilizer that did the trick, helped by the method of planting on ridges and cultivating twice. Anyway they came out as big as or bigger than American sweet potatoes without any disease or insect trouble—local seed also. And the people came and watched me dig and exclaimed. I think at least a hundred people tramped through the vegetables to get to the sweet potato patch and wonder filled their eyes when I would fork up a vine with five or six one-pounders on it. Now if I can store these things there won't be any reason for the people not to plant a lot more of them. . . .

December 14, 1965
Dhankuta

Here I sit once again in Dhankuta, sunning myself on the porch. I came in last Friday with a burned right foot, which didn't bother me at all then, but on Saturday the blisters started coming out and the pain developed with the blisters. On Sunday it got so bad that I couldn't walk, because lowering my foot below the level of the rest of my body would produce blood pressure which was really intolerable. The Indian doctor came and looked at it and said it looked healthy and had me come to his office yesterday to have the dead skin removed and to have a nice dressing applied. Today the pain still comes when I stand up, but I'm hobbling around pretty well. It all happened last Wednesday night when I was rendering lard from the fat I'd gotten at the market. As I took

it off the fire, I set the round-bottomed pot on the floor with a
stick through the two little metal handles. When I had to go on
the other side of the pot, I guess I stepped on the stick and poured
about a pint of the lard onto my foot. Directly I stepped into a
pail of cold water, which cooled it immediately and I think helped
a great deal. That night the pain was pretty bad, but on Thursday and Friday there was no pain and I thought I was all right.
As it turned out the burn was only skin deep (probably because
of the cold water treatment) and I should be able to go back out
on Thursday. I hope I can get some buffalo meat and suet at the
market here Thursday morning and take it out with me for mince
meat and plum pudding. I'm really anxious to get out there and
get ready for Christmas. Also, since I'll be going to India in January, I've got a lot of work to get caught up on, and to arrange
to have done in my absence. I sure wish I had time to stay there
awhile, but my January vacation is pretty well arranged.

The man from Washington that I came into Dhankuta to meet
never showed up. But I had a lot of other things to do and to buy
anyway. I've also had a chance to meet a few important people
that I hadn't met previously.

When I came in last Friday, Bill Robinson of Group III was
leaving for home. Peggy Day left a few days earlier. This was as
usual an emotion-filled experience. After knowing these people for
the last fifteen months I feel that they are part of my family. Here
we depend very greatly on our few fellow Americans. We really
share our troubles, our desires, our histories and expose our naked
souls to each other, although had we been at home and met we
probably would never even have had a serious conversation with

each other because we have such different interests and back-grounds. But then one day we leave, or they leave, perhaps never to see each other again. But they will be replaced by some other P.C.V.s, quite different, with whom we will once again develop an interdependency, as close and intimate as it is temporary. I have known all but one of the sixteen P.C.V.s who have lived in Dhan-kuta and none of them have been replaceable—each one has left something behind, and taken something with him of the place—all uniquely.

January 1, 1966
Dhankuta

Dear Mom and Dad,
Here it is a New Year. I came down to Dhankuta yesterday on my way to India for a month's vacation. Christmas was a great suc-cess—actually the nicest since I left home. I had had some trouble getting moving, with my burnt foot (which is fine now,) so I was sort of sitting around until about three days before Christmas, when my oven arrived from Dhankuta, along with flour, raisins, spices, nuts, etc. Before this all I had managed had been mince meat, plum pudding and a batch of bread, which didn't rise (it made good stuffing anyway.) I had brought buff meat and suet with me from Dhankuta market the previous Thursday. The [fol-lowing] Thursday night the first guests arrived: Bob and Brian from Dhankuta and Barbara Goldberg who teaches in Dharan. They came while I was popping corn for popcorn balls, but I also

had a pork stew on the fire and whipped up some corn bread in
a hurry. That evening I made fruit cake after everyone was off to
bed. The next day I tried bread again—which rose slightly—we
also made a few cookies, brownies, etc for the party at Larry's
that night. In the late afternoon a porter from Dhankuta arrived
with two young peacocks, five pounds each, and two pounds
of white flour, for pies. He told of an American he had seen on
the trail and we all thought of a boy in Kathmandu who said he
was coming out. Then Vic Mayer came in from the other direction, from Bhojpur, and then it was Christmas Eve. Larry had
an eggnog party for some of the important local people and the
District Governor who was on a village tour. Then we sang carols
until about midnight when I went home and started making
pies—two mincemeat, one cherry, one sour cream, then banana
bread (as long as I was up) and while the pies were baking, one
at a time, I read all about roasting poultry in the *Joy of Cooking*
and then Barbara woke up and had to have a drink of water and
we started wrapping presents and then my rooster crowed and
Santa never quite made it to bed. Then it was time to see about
killing peacocks and peeling potatoes, and off to Larry's house
where Santa Claus appeared for the local children and some of the
other friends. Just before this, while I was out collecting yogurt
(to make cottage cheese) and milk, I got a note from Mac Odell
who was coming with Larry Dornacker from Kathmandu with
two knees that didn't work any more. We sent a horse for them
and they arrived at Larry's just before Santa Claus. Mac had a
better Santa Claus suit with him so Santa made a quick change
(discarding my red flannel night shirt.) About one o'clock we

finally got rid of Santa and brought the Christmas tree back to my house, a beautiful pine which I had carried from Jitpur for two hours. Barb and I took to the kitchen while the rest decorated the downstairs with holly and candles. We put long legs on my bed for a table and borrowed chairs and benches, etc. from the neighbors. About 5:00 Barb and I had everything pretty well accomplished except the peacocks which weren't quite ready so I put on my coat and tie and we went downstairs. The local people, except for five boys were asked to leave. The place was just beautiful with candles on the tree and everything. We even had napkins which I had had a tailor make earlier in the day. There were hors d'ouevres and a bottle of Scotch for those who wanted it. Then we had the Christmas story from the Bible and a couple of carols and then we decided to open gifts since the peacocks still weren't done. Then quick, the peacocks were ready and Barb and I had to rush off and see that everything was hot, gravy made, etc. And then we went downstairs again and were served by the five boys. I cut off a first serving from one peacock and sent the carcass up to the boys and got the replacement, so carving wasn't too difficult. The boys also took care of the mashed potatoes, candied sweet potatoes, cauliflower, stuffing, etc. after we'd had our first serving. We also had cottage cheese salad, pickles, carrots, radishes and cranberry sauce. Since cranberry sauce is not readily available in Nepal, everyone thought of it and we had five cans. Then it was time to devour two of the pies. After all that, we took out the table and chairs, spread blankets on the floor and sang songs and more songs. After completing all the Christmas songs we tried show tunes, folk songs and ended up with rock and roll. Then we had plum pudding flambé and entered into conversation since the cigar smoke would smother any further singing. I dozed off before the rest were finished talking.

The next morning we had waffles and sausage and mince pie. After that the food got scarce and of course people don't like to leave right away when they have to walk two days to get home.

Now I'm on my way to India with Mac—the last of my guests to leave. I'm sure your Christmas was better, but we had a good time too. All the right people (except you) seemed to be there.

Love, Mike

February 11, 1966
Dharan

. . . I went up to Khatare and stayed a week arranging for the chickens and then had to shoot back down here again. On my way up to Dhankuta I stopped in Mulghat at the usual tea shop and I met a group of soldiers starting to get their supper and a couple of government officials that I know, but they seemed rather strange and not as friendly as usual. I didn't stay overnight since it was crowded and I didn't have my sleeping bag. I found out later that the Crown Prince [Birendra] was disguised as one of the soldiers. Had I stayed there I probably would have had a long talk with him. He was just sort of roaming around the country getting to know the people and the situation. In Dharan he stopped in to get some kerosene from the local rationing office and they really gave him a rough time, not knowing he was the Crown Prince. . .

February 28, 1966
Khatare

. . . I guess a lot has happened since I last wrote to you, but I can't remember any of it. I guess I was in Dharan getting chickens. Well, I got them—150 of them. The farm had two crates for carrying them made, like a cabinet with three shelves--all out of light plywood and chicken wire. When we put these on two of the porters, the slanting of the men's backs tipped the shelves too much so that the chickens all slid forward in a pile. We decided to forget the crates and use local baskets for all seven of the porters' loads and mine also. Barbara scrounged up some chicken-carrying baskets (called "koongi") and we put off our leaving until the next morning. I got up at four, got the chickens fed and watered by lamp-light and into their baskets and got the porters off about five and went back to bed, planning to leave a little later and catch up with them. Well, I went to try once again to get kerosene and in spite of my light skin and Barbara helping me, I was unable to get any from the government control and I decided I didn't want to buy from the black market. We were desperate for kerosene and still are—I have about a cup left. It started raining so I never left that day but the next morning I loaded up the remaining thirty birds and went to Dhankuta where I met my porters. There we arranged it so I didn't have to carry a basket any more. Again I sent the porters off before dawn in the same manner and ran around town doing things—getting medicine so I could immunize the chickens, etc. and finally left about noon with a former student of mine who wanted to visit me in Khatare. We caught up with the porters just before sunset and passed them, reaching home about eight. Then we cooked rice for ourselves and seven porters—fourteen cups—and waited around and finally went to bed. They arrived at one o'clock, so I got up and unloaded them and gave them supper. Seven chickens died on the road and then two more. I've been selling chickens (about sixty so far) and trying to get feed for the ones that are left. I finally managed a mash: two parts ground corn, two parts millet, two parts rice bran, one part ground, roasted soybeans, one part mustard oil meal. I also give them buttermilk to drink whenever I can get it. So they are doing all right now. I expect I will get rid of the chickens until all the hens are gone and I'll have forty or fifty roosters to raise myself. Lots of fun.

Now, the biggest news here is that Beverly has come to join Larry and me. This has sort of meant a lot of fooling around getting her set up with a house and all, but Larry took care of most of it. She started eating with me yesterday and will continue until we get her stove built. It is sort of nice having someone to eat with again after so long just cooking and eating for myself. It is sort of refreshing to have a girl around also, especially one who is fresh from the States. She was an Animal Husbandry major so we talk about the chickens—perhaps she will take over my job in a small way when I leave.

I got the package of oats that you sent when I came trough Dhankuta—the oats spilling out all over. The other package you sent has not yet been heard of. If you send me any other package, send it to Kathmandu--include Gillette blue blades, Old Spice shaving mug refill and jockey shorts. I planted some of the oats (what kind were they?) in cooler shadier places where the corn doesn't grow so well. I want to get a lot of seed for next year.

My wheat is looking beautiful and I hope to harvest it within a month.

Give my regards to everyone. I'll be seeing you.

Love, Mike

March 11, 1966

Khatare

Things here are fine, going pretty slowly. Most of the people around are busy planting corn or having marriages, so they don't bother me very much. I've gone to a couple of the weddings also. I went to one last night and watched the ceremony (what there was of it) and the dancing and came home about eleven when the moon came up so that we could walk back without flashlights. It is really hard for me to stay awake after nine o'clock anymore. Gorkha Bahadur—who has become my semi-servant—stayed there all night long, dancing and singing, I expect. This morning when I got up I found my big rooster missing, the one I had traded a pair of my little chickens for. He had been under a basket in front of the house and we had forgotten to put him inside when night came. We went off to the wedding without noticing he was there. So this morning we found a bloody basket and a bunch of feathers lying around. Probably a dog [did it]. . . .

I've got a good chance for a job with U.S.A.I.D. here in Nepal after I finish the Peace Corps. They are planning to hire six ex-Peace Corps Volunteers as what they call Agriculture Development Interns. It would be pretty interesting work, although a lot

Village girls and boys. (Mike Frame)

more hectic than I am used to. Probably not as hectic as going
to college, though. It seems that it would take me a long time to
get through college and I guess I'd better do what I want to now,
while I still have the chance. This country isn't going to wait for
me while I get an education and I think I can be just as useful
without, since so much of what is studied there isn't very relevant
here anyway. Financially, it wouldn't hurt me much to receive
$7,200 per year. . . . A couple of years of that would put me in
good shape to buy the north twenty acres of your farm and start
farming it—intensively. . . .

Well, Beverly is taking care of the new horse and thank goodness she knows what she's doing. I've started writing an ency-
clopedic report about village agriculture and my ideas about

development possibilities. It's going to be long; corn alone took three pages.

Hope you are all well and happy.

Love, Mike

April 4, 1966

Khatare

I went to Dhankuta last Thursday for market and for getting my wages. There I got two letters from you, one from Mary Ellen and one from David. I also got your Christmas box and one from M.E. so I'm having a great time eating goodies. It is really too bad that I haven't gotten your other package from six months ago— I've tried just about everything, except I didn't have the letter from Customs when I went to Calcutta when I could have at least investigated it. I guess we put too many eggs in one basket.

Lately I've been harvesting wheat and I had a real good crop. It was good work, cutting the wheat, tying it in bundles and a couple days later smashing the bundles against a rock. It is also nice to have people come and tell me how good it is and that they want to grow it next year. I've decided to sell the wheat for seed to the local government and give the money to the school. There will be three or four bushels and that will be over ten dollars for the school--enough to pay one of the lesser teachers for a month. That will still leave some wheat for me to eat. Anyway I can see now why the Ag. department is having a big program to grow more wheat. There is a better chance for a wheat crop in the winter than their corn crop in the spring, both water-wise and time wise, but the people are used to growing corn, although it doesn't produce very well and often dries up altogether.

Lately I've gotten about a hundred pounds of bones that I've got mixed with brush, ready to burn and it will make a great big stinking bonfire but it is good fertilizer here where there is a phosphorous deficiency.

A couple days later.
I guess you are probably interested in what I am going to do, come September. As I was telling you in a previous letter, there is a job waiting for me with U.S.A.I.D. The picture has changed slightly, however; I would not be a member of a group of interns, but a Junior Technical Trainee or something like that. I would be a regular employee of A.I.D. at the F.S.R. 7/1 level so you can look up what my pay might be. They seem to tell me that I can work pretty much in whatever part of the Ag program I feel most comfortable in. So it would probably be in Agronomy. I would be living in Kathmandu, but I expect I would be traveling around Nepal. As for coming home, I can certainly do it in September but if possible I will try to put the trip off until Christmastime, after I have a good start on the new job. This job would be for two years with probable advancement. There could possibly be a training program in Washington, D.C.

Now, I don't expect I will want to spend too many years working for A.I.D. I expect it will be too hard on my nerves. But as I see it, I can save a little money for a couple years and then I'd like to buy a little bit of your farm—like the north ten-acre pasture

Farm in the hills. (Mary Ellen Frame)

where I could live off the land. Many people are going to laugh at me when I try to farm on a small scale, pretty much self-sufficiently, but I think it can be done quite easily, that is I think it would be an easy life compared to the businessman-farmer who spends his time juggling his debts, keeping his books, going to meetings and fixing his machinery. He doesn't have much time to really farm, and that's what I want to do and always have wanted to do. So what if I get a backache.

I guess that's all I have to say for now.

Thanks for the fruitcake!

April 17, 1966
Khatare

. . . Give my love to Willy and Sandy. I was just thinking that if
Willy has a problem with weight, what he needs is a good case
of worms. If you have the right kind of worms, they don't bother
you very much; you have a tremendous appetite and although you
eat all you like, you still lose weight. One overweight girl I knew
had worms and the doctor sent her some medicine, but she didn't
take it for a couple of weeks while she lost twenty pounds. But
be careful to get the right kind of worms. Hook worms are hard
to get rid of (you have to take a pill which has the same effect as
drinking a fifth of Scotch). Round worms may give you gas or
make you vomit, or both. Pin worms aren't so bad. Just make sure
you get your worms from a reputable dealer—not from flies!

June 13, 1966
Khatare

Dear Folks,
Last year the monsoon started on June 12, but this year we have
had no rain yet and the countryside is pretty grim. With a poor
rice crop last year, and now with only half, or perhaps less, of
a corn crop, it is pretty hard to get anything to eat. The corn is
drying up pretty badly, although some of the earlier-planted corn
is ripe, while other corn is only knee high. There hasn't even been
enough water to plant the rice seed beds which should have been

planted a month ago. This morning I plowed a big piece of land and we are working it up and making ridges. After the rains start, we can plant sweet potatoes without any further land preparation. Last year I waited until after the monsoon started, to make the ridges, but it was about ten times as hard as doing it before the ground is water-logged. I plowed down some green manure and some horse manure on one piece, also bone meal and I expect excellent results, although it is poor land. I expect well over 200 bushels to the acre. On a patch that I prepared yesterday I did a soil test and where last year most of my land did not even show on the scale, it was so poor, this year that one patch, at least, was only slightly low in phosphorous. I gave it a little bone meal. . . .

I got back from Kathmandu the day before yesterday and I am now all cured and I feel great. The British hospital [in Dharan] could only find hookworm in my stools, but the American doctor in Kathmandu was able to find amoebas and Giardia Lamblia (what I came home with last time) as well as the hook worm. Even so I could still walk thirty miles in a day.

We are getting some fruit now, piles of bananas, all different kinds. The big ones sell for just ten elevenths of a cent. Think I can afford a whole bunch? We don't get such good mangoes here as down on the plains, but today I got a lot of real good plums. Little sour peaches are also available now—they make delicious jam.

I guess I'll be seeing you pretty soon.

Love, Mike

July 1, 1966
Khatare

The plane never came, so I didn't go to Kathmandu and I guess I'll only go now if the helicopter comes after me. I had a terrible trip down to Leghuwa Ghat—quite exciting carrying a forty pound pack (things I wanted to take to Kathmandu and be rid of) and sliding around the rice paddies (in proper English, "the paddy fields.") Then up the river for the most exciting crossing I've ever made. They no longer use dugout canoes; now they have some flat-bottomed long boats, which hold about a dozen porters and the four boatmen with paddles. The boat is swept about a half a mile downstream by the rough water (I've seen the ocean with lower waves.) It is probably the cheapest thrill of its kind in the world— only seven cents. Then when I reached the other side I had to race a mile downstream because I was late for the plane—which never came. I remained all day, thinking I would give them a chance the next day, and so I stayed overnight in the house of a caste which is new to me. It was a Majhi family. They are the caste which runs the boats on the river and also do quite a bit of fishing. Their home-made fishing nets are pretty fantastic, circular, with half–inch mesh and sinkers around the sides. The net is whirled around and thrown so that it lands flat on the water and sinks to the bottom. After some time, it is pulled out by the cord attached to the center and the fish are caught in the folds around the edges. The day I stayed there, they didn't catch any fish so I had to eat poor man's food.

The next day I gave the plane until noon to come and then I started back. Man, it is hot down there when the sun shines. I had to jump into the cold river several times. Then it was drizzling all the way home through the rice fields and woods. I didn't carry the pack back. Jeto will take it into Dhankuta from there. He was supposed to be going today so that he would be back with flour before the Fourth of July. We are planning to have brown bread, fried chicken, baked beans, potato salad (if the mayonnaise works out,) jello with bananas, and peach pie. If you want to join us, you'll have to bring your own sandwiches.

It has been raining almost steadily here for the last twenty hours. My guess is about six or seven inches. The stream, which is half a mile away, can be heard constantly, it's roaring so loudly.

The food situation is easing up somewhat with the harvesting of part of the small corn crop. We are still getting lots of bananas and a few mangoes for fruit. I've gotten sort of sick on them today. Dave is here from Ilam, across the border from Darjheeling. I asked him to buy me five pounds of the best grade of tea from there, rated as the best in the world, to take home with me. I'm also trying to talk Beverly into getting a three-quarter Jersey cow from over there. If I was starting again that is what I would do.

Well, this is the first day of my next-to-last month in Khatare and I will hate to leave it more than other places I've lived in Nepal. But I've always hated to change (even leaving Faribo Canning Company at the end of that summer) but I'm glad that I haven't stayed where I was at any time.

I wrote something to send to the Voice, but on re-reading it I decided to just send it to you. You should get a laugh out of it, as Bev did. You may do with it anything which you think is appropriate (here that would mean either starting a fire, or for t.p.)

Love, Mike

July 20, 1966
Khatare

. . . This year's monsoon is sort of strange. I keep working away in my fields getting ready for the rain and when we have a few days without rain, there is lots to do. I keep praying for more rain, so that I can stop work. It is just like at home; when we are out making hay and we work like the devil when we see a big storm coming. We try to get everything taken care of before it rains, but don't quite make it no matter how hard we work. Then the rain comes and, sweet bliss, relaxation with an easy conscience. That's the way it is here too, only the rain never seems to come when I'm feeling most tired. Actually we have had a fairly light monsoon so far, but there is no danger of anything drying out either. . . . Only perhaps half the rice fields have been planted so far. I have three farmers trying improved rice seed this year and so I have to see that it is properly fertilized; without fertilizer it won't do any better than the local. I'm most busy trying to show the importance of growing sweet potatoes. . . .

I got a load of new potatoes the other day from on top of the ridge—8,000 feet and they are nice and big, so now we are living on green corn (the local flint corn is great for roasting and can be used like sweet corn in many dishes) and potatoes. We can also get just a bit of corn flour now, but no rice, wheat flour or sugar is available for the time being.

Beverly went to Dhankuta for a couple of weeks, since there's no school or anything here, so she is trying to get a few things there; I'll send a man in a couple of days. I haven't been to

Plowing with oxen. (Mike Frame)

Mike building silo in Khatare. (Photographer unknown)

Dhankuta for more than a month now. Maybe I'll go one of these days, just for fun. Well, I've got some work cut out for me until I leave, so the end won't drag too much. The local government is planting an orchard so I get pulled in on that although I know absolutely nothing. We have already planted one hundred tangerine trees, and we have oranges, lemons, grapefruit, mangoes, rambutons, papayas, jack fruit and pineapple left. Then I've got this wheat seed to try to distribute before I leave, so that if there is too great a demand, we can get some more. Then Beverly, I hope, will be running my land when I leave, and I am trying to get her a cow. For this and her horse, I would like to build a stone silo, nine feet in diameter by twenty feet high, line it with cement, and fill it before I leave. This I'll start about the middle of August, and leave when it is finished. If things don't go right, I may be a week or two late, terminating.

Love, Mike

August 31, 1966
Khatare

I expect that you are expecting me rather than this letter, but I may be a few days late. I didn't expect to be writing to you again this trip but Bob came out a couple of days ago and will be taking this back to Dhankuta tomorrow.

My problem here is that I have tackled a little too much to do at the last moment. We are building a silo, six feet in diameter and fifteen feet high. When Bob came I got your last three letters, including Dad's telling me not to build a silo, and what kind to make. Well, Bev has a horse, will have a cow, and Jeto has a heifer. There is also no problem of selling a load or two a day [of silage] in the winter. The problem is getting the thing built. We have been getting too much wet weather and we haven't been able to find labor as we should have. Two days we worked well and put up two feet of wall each day, but for this we need one man laying rock, one providing mud and stones, and six or seven carrying rock. But our workmen don't come and when they do it is more likely to be at noon rather than ten o'clock—when they should start. I told Bev I would finish the silo and get a good start on filling it. Filling it will be even more of a job. The bulk of it will be just wild grass cut by hand, but we may bulk it up with some cornstalks. We will also put in part of the sweet potato crop, which should be ready, probably 500 pounds of roots, plus that much again of vines. Then there is a nice patch of giant Napier grass, which is ten feet high—the greatest producer of fodder in India. The tops and leaves will go in the silo, but the nodes will be used for planting.

Beverly is going to live here so I have promised to make her a kitchen downstairs, which means a new stove and chimney. Then we are going to have a stanchion for the cow--none of this rope-tying stuff.

This all means I should be busy until I leave. I plan to fly to Kathmandu on September 15. If I am lucky I can leave there in a week. If they find something in my innards, who knows?

Mary Ellen asked me to come to Chicago and drive home with her, but unless I get through Kathmandu awfully quickly,

I will come straight home since David and Claire will be leaving [for Peace Corps in Malawi.] Perhaps I can get a direct flight from London to Chicago and go through customs there and meet Mary Ellen there for a few minutes anyway. Driving to Minnesota would be nice, but I would end up taking care of the kids since my driver's license is out of style.

It is sort of hard to leave here as it is hard leaving anywhere where I've lived for awhile. Even though I'm getting used to leaving, I've probably felt more at home here than any other place since I was at home. At least I will be kept busy until I leave this time, which is much easier. I will also be invited out for chicken dinner at about three more places. One place I'm counting on is being invited to Jeto's house to eat. He is so low caste that he would never be so presumptuous as to invite me to his house himself, so in order to coax the matter, I gave him a chicken a couple of months ago, telling him to raise it and cut it when he has me to dinner before I go. I'll get Ghorka to remind him of it one of these days.

Well, I'll be seeing you soon anyway. I'll try to let you know as late as possible when I'll be arriving. I don't know anything until I get to Kathmandu.

Love, Mike

Mike and Bhim Rai, 2007. (Mary Ellen Frame)

Return Visit to Khatare, 2004

We left Pokhara by taxi on my sixty-third birthday, the full moon and the last of *Desain* and drove as far as Hetauda. The road was good except between Mugling and Narayanghat, which was badly damaged by the 2003 monsoon and not yet repaired. My companion was NavaRaj Rai, who keeps house for me in Pokhara and is half way through college.

The drive across the Terai the second day was beautiful, with rice harvest just beginning and marigolds everywhere. From Dharan, the Brtish-built road is excellent and goes through Dhankuta all the way to Hile. The area looks prosperous with the houses newly painted and whitewashed for the holidays, the roadsides and gardens neat and tidy.

Hile is not so picturesque. The bazaar is now about a half mile long, with three-story buildings packed on both sides of the road, busy with commerce. The pavement ends in Hile and the dirt road to Siduwa and Basantpur is rough and rutted. Our taxi wasn't doing well with this road so we sent it back and started walking. It was about four o'clock in the afternoon and I thought we might reach Siduwa, but at sundown we still had a ways to go. There are several new bazaars now along that formerly barren stretch and we stopped in a place called Jhorpati and found an adequate lodge with electric lights.

The Milki Dhanda still has some long stretches of nothing but grass, but I missed the groups of porters that used to populate the ridge top. Now most of the goods move on trucks or tractors with wagons and the people ride busses. All the little bazaars which have popped up are collecting places for vegetables brought by basket load from the surrounding villages. There is a huge production of cabbage, cauliflower, radish, peas and other cool weather vegetables that can now be sent by truck to Biratnagar and into India.

From Jhorpati we reached Siduwa in about half an hour with a beautiful view of the mountains most of the way. Siduwa was never very nice or clean. It is far worse now, with mud and ruts and blaring horns from busses and trucks. Tea and a breakfast of chura, tharkare and eggs is about the same as always.

I was rather worried about the next part of the trip since both of my knees have been giving me a lot of trouble. The walk across to Murti Dhunga was little changed since years ago. But then there is the downhill through Yanglabhon and I must say that it is just as big a drop as it always was. The trip down to the Laxmi Khola took a good two hours and my knees wouldn't have lasted much longer.

The good news is that now the woods are full of black cardamom production. About twenty-some years ago, the British research farm at Pakribas started demonstrations of cardamom and alder tree plantations on hillside lands especially by streams where there is plenty of moisture. This has taken off and cardamom is now a major export from the Eastern hills. About the top third of the Yanglabhon downhill slope is all planted to cardamom and it is very beautiful.

Village children. (Mary Ellen Frame)

We reached Gorhka Bahadur's house in Khatare about noon, so rice had to be cooked while we got used to each other in our present incarnations. It had been about twenty years since I had been there. I knew that Gorkha's father had passed away, but I had wondered about his mother. Seeing her sitting there brought the tears to my eyes. She is eighty-one years old now and pretty frail. Gorkha has a wife and four sons, all of whom were home for the holidays. The oldest (married) had been working in Malaysia and plans to go back. Two sons are in college in Dhankuta and the fourth is in high school in Marek. Gorkha's brother died a few years ago so his wife and two children are also living there. There are also Khancha, whose wife has died, and his two sons, and Khanchi, whose husband ran off, and her two sons, all living there, but split into three households. Lots of boys!

Khatare got hit by an earthquake about 15 years ago. There were two deaths and a lot of injuries. Many of the houses were badly damaged so some were rebuilt and others are just gone. The little house I lived in is completely gone. The Subedar's (Umbar Bahadur Adikari's) old house is standing empty with big cracks in the walls and no outbuildings. It looks quite stark. His family, along with Pitumber's and the Bahuns who lived below there, all moved to the Terai.

On our second day there I wandered around in the afternoon by myself and ended up at the stream where I used to bathe almost every day in warm weather. I was all alone in the jungle (all planted to cardamom) and had a nice bath although I hadn't brought any soap or towel. The water hole in which I used to be able to immerse myself, is long gone, but it was still very pleasant.

We stayed two nights in Khatare. There were not many people there that I remembered. Many have left for the Terai or have passed away. More remembered me and some asked about Beverly, Larry and Jim. They were happy to learn that Larry had not been killed in Vietnam, which had been the rumor.

After Khatare, we walked down to the Laksmi Khola and crossed over to the Jitpur ridge. We didn't go all the way up to the Jitpur bazaar (where the market is on Fridays now) but went to Saphu, which is down the hill to the north of the bazaar. That's where Bhim Bahadur Rai lives with his family We were greeted with *thongba* and pork (semi-preserved from *Desain*) and lots of good cheer.

In Khatare we had eaten goat, chicken and fish (from Gorkha's tiny pond) and lots of *eskoos* (chayote) in various forms, guavas and *sel roti* (fried bread) made especially for us. Lots of tea, milk, *dahi* and *chura* (yogurt and beaten rice) and rice, of course. At Bhim's we had resisted the *thongba* at breakfast time, but had pork and chicken and constant *khaja* (snacks) and *thongba* the rest of the day.

Bhim is also growing cardamom in his woods as well as the usual corn, rice and millet in the fields. Bhim's mother is living separately with her widowed daughter-in-law and grandchildren; we visited them in the afternoon and had the inevitable *jaard* (beer), this time with boiled *eskoos* and steamed-in-the-shell soybeans.

On our second evening in Saphu, the local youth club came by. They were rehearsing for Tihar when they would be going around the village caroling, so they put on a performance for us. We had a great time and even I ended up dancing a few steps.

The next morning we had a nice send-off, with Bhim showing us the trail about half way down to Beltar. Along the Arun river is a road partly used by tractors with wagons. This runs more or less from Hile down through Pakribas and along the river as far as the Pilowa Khola. We saw a few tractors tied up in a minor accident at one point, but no moving tractors. There are a lot of porters along this stretch, mostly carrying loads of cardamom south and the usual consumer goods north. There are also quite a few mule trains carrying roughly the same things.

We stopped for *khaja* a couple of times. I bought a bunch of bananas with seeds in them. The woman in the shop said not to spit out the seeds because they are medicine. I told her that I wasn't sick. The loafers at the tea shop were getting off on the pun about a banana with seeds in it. Lots of laughs.

The road is fairly level for miles so we just kept on walking and got into Tumlingtar just before dark. There was no bridge for crossing the Pilowa Khola but there is a nice walking suspension bridge over the Sava Khola just before Tumlingtar.

Ambar Kumal's parents were expecting us, and we stayed at their house. Ambar had called them from Indiana to tell them we were coming. They have a nice comfortable house now. This was Wednesday, November 4th, so I was anxious to listen to the radio and get the election returns. That was the only discouraging thing about the whole trip!

The Kumals made us quite comfortable after the long walk. There was fresh hot buffalo milk in the morning followed by a succession of snacks and meals all day. Besides the kind of food we'd had at other places, we were served roasted corn and sesame *achar* (chutney), but it was still heavy on the meat with the inevitable chicken, pork fresh from the Friday market and three kinds of fish. There also we had three kinds of *jaard* (beer)—rice, corn and millet. Imagine going trekking and gaining weight! I came back several pounds heavier. That's also surprising since I drank the water everywhere we went. Wherever I went there was piped water from far-off springs to almost every household. I think the people are much more healthy now because of this.

We took showers in the bathhouse, washed clothes and went for a walk around the village. We visited the school where a science room and library are under construction with funds that Ambar Kumal is raising in Indiana. We also visited Ambar's brother's and sister's houses and had the inevitable *khaja* and *jaard*.

Tumlingtar has become a busy place with a bazaar, high school and a huge contingent of army and police to protect the airport. Although there is no road to the rest of the world, there is a motorable road from the southern tip of Tumlingtar up through Khandbari to Manibunjung, with land rover-type vehicles, pickups and minibuses. Motorcycles and bicycles are common on the penninsula. There is also electricity from a small hydro plant which worked most of the time we were there.

Friday was market day in Tumlingtar so we had a good tour of the market in the morning. I bought a couple of cakes of brown sugar to take with me. It is the best brown sugar anywhere. I also got some roasted chestnuts and limes to take to Kathmandu. The market was quite like markets of years ago. Perhaps there are more readymade clothes, but mostly it was fruits, vegetables and grains. And just as in years past, there was the self-important semi-official type man telling an old woman selling *ghue* (clarified butter) that she was supposed to sell it by the kilogram and not use her *mana* measure.

The tickets that we had bought in Pokhara for the flight to Kathmandu said 11:45, but when we stopped by the Cosmic Air office in the morning they said the plane would leave at 2:00 p.m. It came at 3:00. We had a nice clear flight to Kathmandu with a view of the mountains most of the way.

So that was our trip. You are probably wondering about the Maoists. Well, wherever we went, the people would warn us about them, saying that they were on the other side of the valley *(khola pardi)*. It seems that there aren't many local people supporting the Maoists. The village people said that they had come by once or twice but hadn't been much of a problem. They were worried about leaving their own villages except to go to the larger towns. I was surprised by how many young people were in the villages. They haven't all left for bigger towns or foreign work. In Tumlingtar the people talked a lot about the area across the Arun Kosi being overrun with Maoists. No one wanted to go over there. Once again, *khola pardi.*

Mike Frame

Mike Frame. (Claire Frame)

GLOSSARY

anna – coin, roughly 1¼ cents
bhat – cooked rice
Brahmin – priestly caste
Chhretri – warrior caste
cos – distance of two or three miles
curd – yogurt
dal – legume, similar to lentil
Desain – ten-day festival in October
ghee or ghue – clarified butter used in cooking
khukuri – a large, curved knife, national symbol of Nepal
kodali – tool used to dig and cultivate soil
Limbu – an ethnic group
momo – a meat- or vegetable-filled dumpling, steamed or fried
malsanpro – small, weasel-like animal
Newar – an ethnic group, their language
paisa – one hundredth of a rupee
Panchayat – governing body
paratha – a fried flat bread or pancake
puja – worship
Rai – an ethnic group
raksi – a distilled liquor
Rana – an oligarchy that ruled Nepal from 1846 to 1951
ropani – one-eighth acre
roti – bread
roti ping – a "non-ferrous ferris wheel," (Mike)
rupee – basic unit of money
Sherpa – an ethnic group; by extension, one who porters by
    profession

Subedar – an officer in the the Nepali army between Jemadar and
 Lieutenant in rank
thongba – alcoholic beverage made with fermented millet
Tihar – festival of lights, following Desain
tole – neighborhood